Partnering with a Purpose

A Practical Guide to Using
Strategic Alliances to Achieve
Your Business Goals

Dave Koester

with
Charles Hamlin

authorHOUSE®

AuthorHouse™
1663 Liberty Drive
Bloomington, IN 47403
www.authorhouse.com
Phone: 1-800-839-8640

First published by AuthorHouse 8/11/2011

ISBN: 978-1-4567-5103-6 (e)
ISBN: 978-1-4567-5104-3 (dj)
ISBN: 978-1-4567-5106-7 (sc)

Library of Congress Control Number: 2011907846

Cover illustration by Sharon Koester Smith

Printed in the United States of America

To my wife Carol and
my business partner and friend Charley,
who understand my vision, support my goals and
without whose help this book would
not have been possible

Table of Contents

Foreword

"The implementation was flawed, but the strategy was sound." Oh, if only I had a nickel for every time some CEO said this, or words to this effect, in response to criticism over a failed business venture. And yet, only 12-18 months previously, this same CEO was clamoring for a microphone to say things like, "ushers in a new era for [insert company name here]", "poised for growth" and this oldie but goodie, "well-positioned to compete in today's global economy." How often do these strategies, created by no small amount of business brainpower, go awry or downright implode due to a poor implementation?

In today's global market, opportunities abound for creative thinkers who are willing to take on acceptable levels of risk. And many times the quickest, most cost-effective way to pursue these opportunities is by partnering with another company. Strategic partnerships or business alliances can be the best road to expanding your business, particularly in light of today's economic climate where investment capital is tight or in many cases non-existent, combined with limited and strained resources. Strategic partnerships can provide an effective means of expanding your own capabilities by leveraging the core competencies of your partner(s) without the huge costs associated with mergers and acquisitions. They have proven effective in areas such as the development of new product technologies, oil and gas exploration, economic revitalization in foreign countries and, more recently, development and implementation of security standards and procedures for safeguarding people, facilities and information.

But the purpose of this book is not to extol the virtues of strategic partnerships, nor to sell you on the idea that partnering is the one and only way your business can survive in the 21st century. Too many trees have already given their lives in that pursuit, the result being daily announcements, accompanied by the mandatory trumpet-blowing, of new business partnerships, strategic alliances, consortiums, joint ventures and other business relationships that promise to turn our economy on its ear and improve the very fabric of our existence.

And yet, despite our shared belief that partnerships can, in the right context, be successful in reducing product development time, optimizing sales and marketing resources, increasing customer satisfaction, growing market share and any of a number of other business objectives, why is it that 90% of established business partnerships fail to meet their objectives in just the first year? Why aren't there more examples of successful partnerships? And if the failure rate is so high, why do we continue to view partnering as a viable strategic alternative? Are there consistent characteristics among partnerships that succeed? And among those that fail?

In looking for answers to these questions, I reviewed not only my own first-hand experiences with partnerships, but I also spoke with hundreds of business professionals about their own partnering experiences, and I researched numerous publications and books related to partnerships, joint ventures and strategic alliances.

In my research I analyzed partnerships from their very inception, focusing on the original business objectives, the reasons for choosing to go the partnership route, the processes used for analyzing and selecting partners, and the development and implementation of the partnership relationship itself. I zeroed in on key players involved in both successful and unsuccessful partnerships to see if I could uncover the core drivers of their success or failure.

Every partnership I examined had its own story – different industries, each with their own unique supply chain structure, varying histories of the companies and people involved, and vastly different business objectives for each partnership created. But in sifting through this data,

I discovered some recurring themes - steps taken, or not taken - that significantly contributed to the results generated by the partnership.

Some of the most valuable intelligence I've been able to gather deals with lessons learned from partnerships that failed. By asking key people involved, *If you had to do it over again, what would you do differently?* I learned that the same types of mistakes were being made across all forms of business partnerships, regardless of industry or the specific companies involved.

That's when I got the notion that this book should focus on the "how" of strategic partnering. So I set out to develop a guide for developing and managing successful partnerships. A guide that's not only practical and helpful, but also a quick and easy read for today's overloaded business professional.

Within these chapters you'll find, condensed and to-the-point, the "make-sure-you-do-this" and "watch-out-for-that" of planning, developing and implementing an effective business-to-business partnership - one that has clear goals from the outset and is designed and managed to produce successful, real-world results.

But beware! After reading this book and following the guidelines I've laid out, you won't have the "sound strategy, failed execution" crutch anymore. What you will have is a level of implementation excellence that will actually serve to uncover weaknesses in a strategy that may not have been noticed until full market rollout. Identifying these problems earlier in the process will save you exponentially versus discovering them later.

And so it is my ultimate goal that you see such a return on your investment of time and money in this book that it becomes not only a handy guide you'll refer to often, but that you also see it as a worthwhile investment for your co-workers, your employees, your business associates and yes, especially your partners.

Chapter 1 – Why Partner?

In the Beginning...

Og just couldn't seem to get it right. No matter how many times he tried, he couldn't get his stone axe to do anything more than make a big noise and a small dent in the bark of a tree. All of the stone axe heads he carved were either too brittle, and broke on impact, or weren't sharp enough to have any effect at all. You see, this whole working with stone thing was pretty new to Og.

Now, the wooden handle for the axe? That was no problem. Og was very used to working with wood, and over time he had become very skilled. He would find broken tree limbs on the ground and rub them against boulders until they took on the desired shape. No one could match Og's wooden spears, digging tools or clubs. So, making a short wooden handle to which he could attach the stone head of his axe was a breeze. Og's axe handle turned out nice and smooth, felt comfortable in his hand, and was strong enough to perform under those brutal Ice Age conditions. Even his buddy Gra from two caves down would stop by, pick up Og's axe handle, and marvel at the fine craftsmanship.

You see, Gra couldn't make a wooden axe handle to save his life. His handles would always splinter upon impact, or they would gouge poor Gra's hands to the point where it hurt too much to drag them around on the ground. It was a shame too because, even though Gra couldn't make anything useful out of wood, he was a wiz when it came to working with stone. Gra had taken to working with stone the way a baby mastodon

1

takes to water. Cranking out stone axe heads that were both strong and sharp was no problem for a caveman of Gra's talents.

So one fateful day, they both became so frustrated trying to cut firewood with their inferior axes (every respectable cave simply *had* to have fire), that they were ready to quit evolving altogether. It was on that day that they got together, grunted it over, and decided to make a trade. Og would make an extra wooden axe handle and give it to Gra in exchange for the extra stone axe head that Gra would make.

Soon they were both chopping away with the finest axes anyone had ever seen. Well, it didn't take long for some of the others to come by and, amazed at what they were seeing, offer mammoth meat, hides and other bounty in exchange for either Og's or Gra's axe.

The two stopped their chopping and looked at all of the fine merchandise being offered (the cave wall paint set was especially cool). They looked at their axes, scratched their sloping foreheads, and then looked at each other. And so it was that in that moment, Og & Gra, the world's first strategic partnership, was born.

Cheesy I know, but who's to say I'm wrong? The point is, business-to-business strategic partnering has been around for a very long time. It has been, and will continue to be, an effective way for businesses to compete and to grow.

Not just a fad, 'cause it's been goin' on so long

From the song, "Catch a Wave" by the Beach Boys

Surprisingly, Brian Wilson was referring to surfing here, and not strategic partnering. But like surfing, partnering has also been around quite awhile, and in both, the object is to stay afloat, not wipe out, and don't forget to watch out for sharks. Strategic partnering is not, as some have said, only a recent and temporary phenomenon, doomed to suffer the same fate as pet rocks, leg warmers, and three-piece suits (I refuse to give mine up; they shall return!) From Og & Gra to Ben & Jerry*, strategic partnerships have always been a vehicle for real business growth.

But strategic partnering, in all its various forms, has seen a significant increase over the last few years. Businesses looking to expand their product lines, access new sales channels, complement their R&D efforts or reduce the overall risk of a new business venture, are turning to strategic partnering in greater and greater numbers as a cost-effective means of meeting their growth objectives. And you don't have to look very far to see why business partnerships are more popular now than ever.

The Climate is Right

Consumerism, a relatively recent addition to the American lexicon, is defined as a preoccupation with and an inclination toward the buying of consumer goods. The rapid spread of this condition in the U.S. in the 1990s and 2000s has led to higher and higher settings for the bar of global competition. From a macroeconomic perspective, consumerism has trumped nationalism as a driver of purchasing behavior. Seeing *Made in America* on a product is just not as crucial a selling point for U.S. consumers today like it used to be. In short, we don't just want more stuff - we want better stuff faster and less expensive, and we're not too particular about where it comes from.

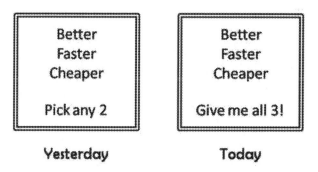

U.S. businesses, refusing to give up precious market share without a fight, have shifted manufacturing jobs, along with many other functions, to other countries in an effort to compete with new market offerings from abroad.

I know. You're not here for an economics lesson. But when we connect the dots, we see businesses today focused on product quality and cost control as never before. Stories in the news about companies downsizing…excuse me, "rightsizing" (how come no one ever rightsizes upward?) are so commonplace that they've stopped raising eyebrows. And instead of being taken as a sign that a business may be struggling, news of all this payroll slashing is usually followed by an upsurge in the company's share price and bonuses for all the executives (Hey, this is great! Let's do it again!)

But businesses are like plants - they both need to grow in order to survive (insert your own fertilizer joke here.) So with all this dieting to cut corporate fat going on, how are we going to grow our business and still control costs? From a resource standpoint, how can we leverage growth opportunities when we uncover them without taking on too much risk? We're all asked to "do more with less" these days, but how far can that really take us?

A Look in the Mirror

In response to these many challenges, business leaders today are looking at more creative ways to meet the needs of both customers and shareholders. CRM initiatives, streamlined logistics, asset refinancing, employee empowerment and quality control programs are just some examples.

Add to this list outsourcing, which began with back-office functions such as facilities management, real estate, HR and supply chain management. But now outsourcing is reaching into more core functions like engineering, customer service, and even manufacturing. Companies are looking at themselves in the mirror and asking questions such as, "If our core strength is our superior product design and engineering, why are we spending so much maintaining such a large customer service group? Could this function be performed better by someone else?"

A shift in traditional business thinking, to be sure. For the most part, senior managers no longer see an inherent advantage in directly controlling every aspect of their product's journey through production and into the hands of their customers. Rather, they're taking a hard look at all functions and asking themselves how they could be done better. And that's what's key here. Outsourcing is being driven not only from cost-cutting measures and the desire to squeeze every ounce of water out of that rock as possible. It also offers a way to significantly improve the overall product or service by utilizing another company's experience and expertise.

Advancements in technology are also fueling the outsourcing machine. Information and communications technologies have developed around sharing information and creating more efficient workflows, enabling a more mobile and more productive workforce. Technology that allowed people to start working from their homes in the 1990s is now more advanced and is enabling people from all over the world to work together on the same project simultaneously. So now your boss can tick you off from halfway around the world the same as if he or she were just down the hall. That's progress!

It's Still About the Benjamin's

But despite enhancing a business' overall capabilities, enabling technologies and streamlining processes, outsourcing still would not be so popular if it weren't for the significant cost-saving opportunities it can offer. Let's face it - it's difficult for a division VP in the U.S. to justify an in-house engineering staff at an average salary + benefits cost well in the six-figures when the same skill set could be provided from elsewhere for less than half the cost. Savings like these are awfully hard to ignore, especially when they can help free up capital necessary to invest in new product innovations.

I'm writing this at the end of 2009, and the outsourcing engine is running on all cylinders (with imported parts, of course.) The U.S. economy, after experiencing four consecutive quarters of negative growth in GDP, has slooooooowly started to grow again. The result? A net loss of 3.6 million jobs over the last 13 months. Many economists are calling the return to modest growth a *jobless recovery*, meaning that even though the economy is showing signs of life again, the job growth has not followed.

Much of this can be explained by increases in worker productivity. We're all learning to do more with less (except for us consultants, who never did anything to begin with.) Even as business levels start to pick up, managers are using technology and squeezing their existing staff for all they're worth before going to the well to ask for additional people. Makes total sense, but it still begs the question: How can we make the quantum leaps necessary to stay competitive into the future when we've got the pedal matted now just keeping the place running?

Weapon of Choice

When looking at strategic alternatives for growing their companies, many business leaders are turning to partnerships. Partnerships are more popular today than ever because they offer significant advantages over other growth alternatives such as acquisitions or developing new capabilities completely internally.

Here are just some of the advantages of strategic partnering:

- Reduced risk
- Compensate for weak areas within your company
- Speed to market for new products
- Expanded product line
- Cost savings versus developing the new capability internally
- Access to new technology
- Offer a more comprehensive solution and value proposition
- Access to new sales channels
- Streamlined R&D effort
- Allows you to focus on your core competencies

So by looking at the state of the business world today and the many advantages offered by strategic partnerships, it's easy to see why so many business leaders believe that partnerships and strategic alliances are the greatest things since stock options (Yes, even sliced bread is finding it hard to compete these days.)

Now the Bad News

Before you start signing up partners and writing those press releases, consider this: studies of strategic partnerships have shown that over the first 2-3 years of the partnership, 9 out of 10 fail to meet their objectives. When I first read that, I thought, *That just can't be right.* And yet, in studying profiles of past partnerships and talking to colleagues engaged in partnering, I became convinced that this failure rate was pretty accurate. It's sad but true - an overwhelming majority of partnerships do not live up to expectations.

Reasons for this are many – lack of commitment from management, the partnership was poorly structured, no clear communications protocols, no defined conflict resolution process and lack of accountability to name a few. In studying past partnerships I noticed that in many instances, management felt the new partnership was such a good fit, and the newly created value proposition would be so compelling to customers, that the partnership would just succeed on its own without too much "meddling" from them.

But what they viewed as meddling, I would characterize as commitment and involvement. We'll cover this in more detail a little later, but it bears mentioning up front: Without strong, on-going commitment from senior management, partnerships, no matter how well formed, are doomed to fail. You'll notice this as a recurring theme in this book.

Not to be overly dramatic about it, but the road to a successful partnership is strewn with many potholes – not to mention broken glass, confusing traffic signs and speed traps. And if you're not very careful, you'll end up broken down by the side of the road, or even worse, as road kill. Aren't you glad I didn't get too dramatic?

Do Not Walk Softly

Partnering with a Purpose takes commitment, understanding, a willingness to look in the mirror and perhaps most significantly, the ability to embrace new business development opportunities in a non-traditional fashion. Sound difficult? Well it is, and it will challenge the very core, history, culture and methodology of even the best-managed organizations. The results of an effective, well-structured strategic partnering model can translate into significant gains for both organizations, but it doesn't come without recognizing that both companies must be willing to embrace change and trust one another with no hidden agendas.

So take heart – partnering may not be as easy as you thought, but the rewards from doing it the right way will probably go beyond even your best expectations. Even by reading this book you're demonstrating an elevated level of commitment to partnering the right way – in other words, commitment to Partnering with a <u>Purpose</u>. This commitment needs to be the very first ingredient into our partnership bouillabaisse. The next step will be a hard look in the mirror through something I call: The Strategic Readiness Exam.

Chapter 2 – Are You Really Ready For This?

So now we know that strategic partnerships, successful ones anyway, take a serious amount of effort and commitment. It stands to reason that organizations considering using partnerships as a means to grow would want to maximize their chances of success. And the first step towards success is taking a hard look within your own organization to determine your readiness level to enter into a strategic partnership.

Please Don't Make Me Look

Nobody likes to look at himself or herself in the mirror too closely because when you do, that's when all the flaws, imperfections and scars become all too visible. As I got older I found myself standing further and further away from my bathroom mirror. When I finally hit the back wall of my bathroom and could get no further away, fortunately that's when my eyesight started going. It's funny how the worse my eyes get, the better looking I become.

But look closely in the mirror we must, for Partnering with a Purpose requires, at least for most organizations, a severe paradigm shift. It demands that we look at many aspects of our business: products, employees, competitors, suppliers and yes, even customers, in an entirely new light. These changes need to occur before any type of partnership, or potential partner candidates, are even considered. And don't think that just because you've got the words "willingness to embrace change" somewhere in your mission statement that you're good to go. The type of change we're talking about starts at the top and permeates throughout the entire organization.

The Strategic Readiness Exam

If you're like me, the word "exam" or "test" brings on its own special kind of anxiety attack, complete with cold sweats and visions of the Four Horsemen of the Apocalypse pulling into your driveway. But before you start preparing your cheat sheet (I was amazed at how many chemical formulas I could fit on a 3x5 index card), consider this: The only way you can truly fail this exam is by not being totally honest. Any spin you try to put on your answers will only reduce your chances at ultimate partnering success. Be as honest with yourself as you can as you go through the exam. This will allow you to clearly identify what changes need to be made within your organization to optimize the chances of achieving a successful partnership.

So remove the rose-colored glasses, and let's take out a Number 2 pencil and get started.

> **QUESTION 1 –** *Does your senior management team embrace a common understanding of the definition of strategic partnering and its expected results and, more importantly, are they willing to get involved in the process?*

I know we've touched on this before, but it bears repeating – senior management must be on board with this process or it will fail. And when I say "on board" I don't just mean showing up at kick-off meetings or press conferences to make a speech. I mean setting reasonable goals, chairing progress meetings, holding people accountable and, most importantly, spreading the partnership gospel throughout the organization.

Partnering can be a difficult concept for some execs to get their heads around. Most organizations are founded and built upon hard work, determination and a powerful vision of the future. The beliefs and values of the founders get distilled and reinforced throughout the organization as it grows. The executive team must be shining examples of these values. New employees become indoctrinated into "our way of doing things." And I bring this up not to be critical in any way. On the contrary, the "we can do anything if we put our minds to it" mentality has served businesses well and will continue to do so in any economy. But it can make accepting the concept of partnering a bit more challenging. The idea that another organization might be better equipped to handle certain functions or take on specific responsibilities will be difficult for many of your employees to swallow. So it's critical that the management team be united in their commitment to partnering as a channel for profitable growth.

As far as having a common understanding of the definition of strategic partnering and its expected results, here is a classic definition of what a strategic alliance is:

An Alliance is a formal relationship that is strategic or tactical between two or more parties having compatible or complementary business interests and goals to pursue a shared interest or to meet a critical business demand for their mutual benefit.

Note my use of the word "formal" in the definition. Obviously, there is an entire spectrum of business-to-business relationships, from a handshake verbal agreement on up. But for our purposes, we'll only be considering legalized, formal relationships. Building a relationship upon a legal foundation makes it easier to share capital to fund research, or develop and market new products. Also, formalizing the alliance increases the level of commitment for both sides, and minimizes any misinterpretation of the terms of the relationship.

QUESTION 2 – *Can your company, once the non-disclosure and confidentiality agreements are in place, really operate with a true trust imperative?*

This question challenges your organization to freely share information with your partner. Not an easy task for any organization, especially in today's economy where information equates to power. I mean who, after all, enjoys airing their own dirty laundry? And yet, by speaking openly of your own company's strengths *and weaknesses* with your partner, that is where the largest opportunities for growth can reveal themselves.

And yes, this information sharing can extend to operating data, financial pro forma, etc. Can't you just feel the hairs on the back of your neck rising? I told you this wouldn't be easy. But think about it: Everything you'd like to know about your partner, they will also want to know about you. We'll cover the partner evaluation process in a later chapter, but if your organization guards its information like Fort Knox, and would never dream of sharing it with "outsiders", this should send up a red flag. Senior management needs to understand going in that sharing key information plays an important part throughout the entire partnering process. It is a key component of the trust imperative.

Of course there are sensitivities around certain information. This is what confidentiality and non-disclosure agreements (NDA) are made for. Crafting a proper NDA at the outset of a business relationship will provide both companies the security and protection they need to openly communicate with each other.

QUESTION 3 – *Can you and your company avoid the "hidden agenda" syndrome?*

This question is closely related to Question 2 and deals with openly sharing information and putting all cards, and concerns, on the table.

As mentioned before, a strategic alliance with another company might be perceived as a threat by some within your own organization. Perhaps the new partner is especially strong within a particular function. The head of that same function within your own company might feel threatened or at least a bit defensive. This could motivate some, while showing nothing but support and saying all the right things at the meetings, to work behind the scenes to torpedo the partnership before it has a real chance at success.

Now there's no need to go Sherlock Holmes on everyone in your office – looking for suspicious behavior and tapping phone lines. But this is something you definitely need to be aware of. You need to answer this honestly: Is your company willing to openly share and exchange all necessary information to support a collective business development strategy, or will personal egos and agendas get in the way?

Most of the partnership failures related to this question happen because the champion(s) within the two organizations did not enroll the key players to support the partnership. Therefore it's critical that a vision of success be developed and communicated early and often to key people – not just those who will be directly involved with the partnership - but also those who could undermine the partnership and hurt its chances of success.

"…and I've lied and I've cheated at cards. But the one thing I ain't never done – I never gulled a partner. 'Cause the one thing sacred even to low scuff like me, is a man's partner."

Lee Marvin from the movie, "Paint Your Wagon"

QUESTION 4 – *Is your company willing to make the necessary investments to train and educate your employees and your strategic partner?*

Picture in your mind your ideal partnership. You've found the exact partner you were looking for. You've hit upon an incredible new value proposition that will transform the entire marketplace. Your alliance will produce layers upon layers of benefits to all mankind. You're picking out which tie to wear to the Nobel Prize dinner and touching up your acceptance speech...but wait! Now the vision changes to your sales rep making a call on one of your regular customers. After reading an article based on your brilliantly worded press release, the customer asks, "What's with this new partnership you're forming with ABC Company?" As the tension mounts, your sales rep replies (drum roll please), "I don't know. They never tell us anything."

(Fade to black.)

Oh no! You forgot to train your employees! How can we expect the news to spread about our new business venture when even our own people don't understand what it's all about? One of the most important benefits of partnering is access to a whole new network of business contacts. Word-of-mouth endorsements are the most valuable of all. Your new partner can open a myriad of opportunities for you. Isn't that one of the reasons you chose each other?

But it isn't just going to happen on its own. Wheels must be put into motion. Employees on both sides of the partnership need to be well informed and trained on what to communicate to the masses. Believe me, if the strategy is sound and you have the right partner, the investment you make in training will return to you many times over. So we need to make sure up front that there is a commitment of resources to training and employee communication.

"Training is everything. The peach was once a bitter almond; cauliflower is nothing but cabbage with a college education."

Mark Twain

QUESTION 5 – *Are you and your company willing to develop an open communication exchange with your partner?*

Starting to see a pattern here? For a partnership to survive and thrive, communications between the partners must be open, frequent, and at multiple organizational levels. There simply cannot be a single point person for all communications that run between organizations. Yet this is typically what happens. The champions of the partnership for both organizations become very territorial. They start to insist that each and every inter-company communication go through them. If this scenario develops, a communications bottleneck forms, small issues become large problems, and the partnership never gets off the ground.

Here are some examples of partnership communication channels:

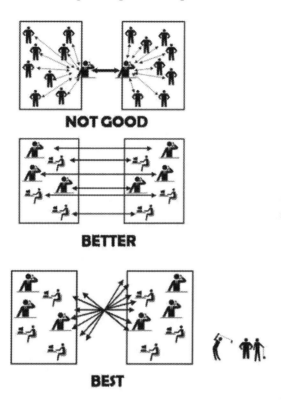

NOT GOOD

BETTER

BEST

QUESTION 6 – *Who's in charge?*

This question might seem a bit cryptic, but it's important that decision-makers be defined up front with respect to the partnership. How will decisions regarding the partnership, or potential partnership, be made? Who is accountable to whom?

Most of this will be determined within your existing organizational structure. But many times a new structure, one that supercedes the existing org chart, needs to be established to support the partnership. The key at the outset is for you to challenge your organization's ability to put non-traditional reporting structures into place. If your company has used cross-functional project teams in the past, then you already have much of the infrastructure and experience necessary to support a partnering initiative.

QUESTION 7 – *Can your organization develop the right strategic business plan to support the alliance?*

"If you fail to plan, then you plan to fail."

Some uptight business guy

Chapter Three discusses the partnership plan in more detail, but it needs to be acknowledged up front by senior managers that a comprehensive business plan is required before entering into any type of formal strategic alliance. This plan must define the mission, vision and strategic objectives of the partnership business venture. Also, this plan needs to detail the expected resource commitment necessary for success. The partnership business plan clearly communicates to all stakeholders exactly the What?, Why?, When?, Where?, How much? and How long? of the partnership. It is a must-have for gaining buy-in and approval.

Again, the lesson here is that no strategic partnership should be entered into lightly. If there are not sound business reasons, and corresponding resource support for the partnership, it should not be pursued further. Lacking a plan, there can be no Partnering with a Purpose.

Not that the plan can't change over time. In fact, it will need to be reviewed and modified on an on-going basis to keep up with ever-changing conditions.

QUESTION 8 – *Are you setting up your partnership with assigned responsibility, but without individual accountability?*

Ah yes. Responsibility with no accountability - Let the finger pointing begin!

Since we're setting up a new organizational infrastructure to support our partnership, there's a definite possibility that divisions of labor will be blurred to the point that many of your people end up with business cards that looks something like this:

The New Company

David R. Koester
Generally-in-charge-of-a-lot-of-things

1-800-dontblameme

Not always a bad thing, mind you. Partnerships generally require people with an entrepreneurial spirit – you know, the type that keeps the main objective in the front windshield and from whose lips you'll never hear, "That's not my job."

The problems begin to arise when progress towards the partnership objectives gets measured (and believe me, it needs to be measured!), and it's determined that some course corrections need to be made. Senior managers need to know where and how to "tweak" the partnership to get it back on course. In other words, you need to have individuals who are going to be held accountable for those specific results. I told you this was not for the faint-hearted.

QUESTION 9 – *Where are the points of linkage between the two companies?*

This is closely related to Question 5, but deals more with the issue of ownership. Typically, partnerships begin with a champion on each side of the fence. These champions then sell the idea of a strategic partnership internally. If they do their jobs well and have all their ducks in a row (ref: PLAN), then nine months later the presidents from both companies deliver a spanking new partnership. Cigars all around.

What will usually happen though is the champions become the sole owners of the partnership by default. Although many will participate, the champions are the ones left holding the bag when the CYA epidemic hits your office. Don't let this happen to you.

Ownership of the strategic alliance needs to be shared with many people on many organizational levels. And not so we have others to blame when things go wrong. It's because ownership is the ultimate motivator for people to do extraordinary work. If I feel like this is <u>my</u> business, I'll be more motivated to, 1) go beyond what's required, 2) look for potential problems down the road, 3) be more open and creative when discussing solutions, and 4) generally be more dedicated to the ultimate success of the entire venture. The more project ownership is shared, the greater the chances are for success.

QUESTION 10 – *How do you avoid the "not invented here" syndrome?*

My, we consultants do like our syndromes, don't we? But this one, closely related to the "hidden agenda" syndrome, is a particularly nasty malady that I've seen destroy partnerships from the inside out.

Case in point: Many retailers were slow to implement an effective Internet-based business model. Not because they didn't have the vision of how the Internet could transform the way people shop, it's because many of them were determined from the outset to build their model completely on their own. And why not? Don't we have quality IS people that have successfully linked hundreds of our store locations nationwide? Why shouldn't we just do this ourselves?

Toys "R" Us, after trying to build an entire Internet distribution system completely on its own, decided instead to partner with Amazon. com. The result? Toys "R" Us had a well-established, highly efficient means of reaching more customers, and Amazon.com had the number one toy retailer as their partner for entry into this highly competitive market.

Remember: No matter what skill sets your partner brings to the table, <u>someone</u> from your company is going to perceive them as a threat.

So Dr. Koester, how do we cure the "not invented here" syndrome?

I'm glad you asked. The underlying causes for this condition deal with lack of assigned responsibility and accountability, silo mentalities and, for the most part, just plain ego. But all of these can be mitigated if the partner companies establish and embrace well-defined rules of engagement, be open and honest in communications, and generally just treat the partnership opportunity as a vehicle for new business development…one that's going to benefit all of you.

Time's Up, Pencils Down

That wasn't so bad, was it? It's doubtful that you were able to honestly answer each of the preceding ten questions without uncovering at least one area of concern. That's quite alright. The purpose of the exam is not to qualify or disqualify your company for a strategic partnership. The objective is to flag as many of the speed bumps and potholes as possible that you're likely to encounter along the way. As you'll see, it's definitely to your advantage to be aware of these issues going in rather than discover the gruesome truth midway through the partnering process. So put away your sawdust, spray paint, deodorizer and any other masking agent you may keep in stock. Hang out that dirty laundry with both pride and determination. If we all know what to expect going in, then we can plan for its contingency and maximize our chances for success.

But the underlying lesson of this exercise is that partnerships cannot be successful unless they are regarded as significant company-wide efforts, with all the due diligence, resources and overall commitment inherent therein. If they are regarded as auxiliary efforts, to be considered only as time allows, then they can never yield the impactful results hoped for. And that's not to say that the partnering effort has to trump all other company priorities. We should expect the need to compete with many initiatives for scarce company resources. However, now you've been armed with many red flags, and you should be prepared to wave them furiously if the need arises.

And so with our eyes wide open, we can now proceed with our partnering endeavor. But how should we proceed? What do we do now? Where should we go? Who do we need to talk to?

It sounds like we need a plan.

Chapter 3 – The Partnership Plan

"All battles are won or lost before they are fought."

Sun-Tzu

"A plan is nothing. Planning is everything."

General Dwight D. Eisenhower

"Do you plan on wearing <u>that</u>?"

My wife Carol the last time we went out

Most of us Homo sapiens are not planners by nature. In fact, most people hate to plan just about anything. I can tell you the planning gene, if such a thing exists, was filtered out of the Koester bloodline long before yours truly entered this world. Beyond where my next beer or round of golf is coming from, I really don't plan for much.

Ok, that's not entirely true. I actually do see the value in having a plan. If nothing else, a plan defines exactly what it is you want to accomplish. Even a daily "to do" list is a form of plan. When I began working out of my house as a consultant, I quickly learned that if I didn't start each morning with a well-defined idea of what I wanted to get done, I'd reach the end of the day with little or no real progress. There are just too many distractions to occupy our time these days, both at work and at home. If we don't keep our eyes on our goals - those objectives that are truly important to us - we can quickly get lost in a fog of activity that leads nowhere.

Plans provide a discipline that helps us define and reach our goals. Whether it's building a successful B2B partnership, getting your golf handicap down to single digits, putting your kids through college or hosting a dinner party, a plan helps get us where we want to go.

The Pain of Planning

So if plans are such wonderful things, why do so many people avoid them like the plague? Well, I'm no psychologist (although I've been referred to many), but it's my belief that people generally don't plan as much as they should because they don't want to deal with any anxiety they might feel if events don't go exactly according to their plan. It's like we think to ourselves: *Why should I bother planning things out when fate is going to take over sooner or later anyway?* After all, when's the last time you remember <u>anything</u> going according to plan? I don't care if it's a military war or a family picnic (interchangeable for some of us), something always happens to mess up the plan.

And yet, it is exactly because things never go according to plan that plans are needed in the first place. Yes, irony indeed. For any worthwhile undertaking, steps need to be defined, timeframes, consequences and contingencies need to be considered. If we start working on Step 4 before completing Step 3, what problems will this cause? If we wake up and it's raining on the day of our outing, what are we going to do then? If our first quarter results were below goal, what adjustments do we need to make? Do we need to change our year-end projections?

With the possible exception of the original charter for Og & Gra, plans are never written in stone. It's quite alright for them to be changed. In fact, you should <u>expect</u> to have to alter your plan throughout execution. Better yet, define up front what it is you're going to do in the likely event that X happens. This is called contingency planning, and it's a good way to define a back-up plan in case our first approach proves to be unworkable.

Contingency planning has been around ever since some prehistoric sea creature decided to see what crawling up on land would be like. No doubt, it thought: *Well if this doesn't work out, I can always just flop back into the water.* See? Without that creature's contingency planning, you might be trying to read this book underwater.

Of course, the main benefit of having a plan is to keep you on track towards your goals. Remember our metaphor earlier about the road to a successful partnership being strewn with potholes, confusing road signs and other such nonsense? Well, think of your plan as a roadmap to help you navigate through the confusion and get you to your destination in one piece. Regardless of what's being thrown at you – changing personnel, new budget reporting guidelines, the "Crisis of the Week," or perhaps the Boss just got back from a conference and now wants everyone in the office to chant the word "quality" for 15 minutes a day – through all of this, your plan can keep you heading in the right direction. Without a plan, you can start out heading for the World Series at Yankee Stadium and end up in a tobacco-spitting contest in Dogpatch (which you end up losing to the local favorite, but only because you have too many teeth).

Begin with the End in Mind

The first part of our Partnership Plan needs to be a statement of our objectives. What do we want to accomplish with this hare-brained scheme of ours? Again, this is a new business venture and needs to be regarded as such. Think of yourself as an entrepreneur with a great idea for a new business. You need to go to a venture capital company to obtain start-up capital. How do you present your case?

Remember, a partnership is not an objective in itself. Partnerships are tools for businesses to use to achieve strategic growth objectives. Think of partnering like the Internet – having a web site is not a strategic business objective – however, using the web as part of a campaign to increase brand recognition 25% is. Or, if you're a technophobe like me, think of partnering as a shovel – you don't wake up in the morning, grab your shovel and say, *I'm going to do something with this shovel today. I have no idea what, but I know I'll be using this shovel.* Before you know it, you find yourself in a deep hole (bad pun intended). The objective is to plant a tree (actually, it's to block the view of our neighbors). The shovel is just a means to this end.

So there need to be underlying business objectives that support the establishment of a strategic partnership. Objectives for your business plan should be as specific as possible. A good format for any business plan objective is the **S.M.A.R.T.** format – make them **S**trategic, **M**easurable, **A**ttainable, **R**ealistic and **T**imely. Here are a few examples:

- Achieve 5% penetration of the European market by Q3 of next year through a series of partnerships with local distributors.

- Partner with a best-in-class service provider with national coverage to offer a comprehensive service package along with our products by the end of next quarter.

- Grow our basic facility management revenues by 15% in the coming fiscal year by expanding our basic service via partnerships to provide one-stop-shopping for all of our customers' facility management needs.

- Increase customer satisfaction to a 95% good or excellent rating by year-end by partnering with a company specializing in training to offer on-going customer training programs focused on using our products to maximize overall customer value.

Here's a few that I would not consider to be SMART objectives:

- Establish a successful partnership with ABC Company.

- Increase sales through distributorships.

- Find a partner to market our products in Canada.

- Leverage external channels to increase market share.

These in the second group have the beginnings of valid objectives, but need to contain more information relative to the SMART criteria in order to hold up under the intense scrutiny from upper management that you're sure to encounter. Remember: a partnership just answers the how; a strategic objective answers the what.

Let's Plan Our Plan

Now that we've defined our core objective(s), let's take a look at other essential elements of our Partnership Plan.

There are many business plan templates floating around, and your company probably has its own preference. At a minimum though, your Partnership Plan should include the following:

I.   Executive Summary

II. Description of Product/Service Offering

III. Market Analysis

IV. Marketing Plan

V.   Operating Plan

VI. Financial Analysis & Attachments

We're not going to go into excruciating details about each element of the Partnership Plan. On the following pages are just some guidelines to help you develop a cohesive plan. The important thing about your plan is that you have one, that it addresses your organizational needs and requirements, and that it lays out a clear direction and end goals for the partnership endeavor.

Executive Summary

The president of a start-up company asked me recently to read over their business plan and offer any suggestions that I might have. They were looking for capital funding and needed a well-crafted business plan in order to attract investors. When I told him I'd be glad to, he handed me a document 38 pages long. I gave it a quick glance and told him I'd concentrate most on the executive summary, since that's all that most people will ever read anyway. Then he said to me, "What you're holding *is* the executive summary. I'll have a copy of the full document printed and sent over to you." My eyes still haven't recovered.

Contrary to popular belief, there are no extra points awarded based on the thickness of your plan. Keep it simple and avoid over-embellishment. Don't load up your basic story with superfluous analysis and irrelevant background. You can do like I did and just save all that extraneous stuff for your book.

This is especially true for your executive summary. A summary is just that – an easily digestible overview of your plan. It should offer simple answers to these questions:

- What exactly are you proposing to do?

- How do you plan on doing it?

- Why is this such a good idea?

- How much is it going to cost?

- What is the expected return for the company?

- What are the major risks involved?

If it takes you more than five pages to answer these questions, then your executive summary is probably too long.

Description of Product/Service Offering

Here's part of the plan where you can go into some detail about what the new partnership is going to bring to the marketplace. Define the basic customer need for your offering and how your product or service is going to meet that need. Will your offer be a "me too" and meet the defined need in much the same manner as currently available products/services, or are you bringing something completely new to the competitive arena?

And since you've decided that a strategic partner will be needed to help market and/or deliver your product/service, here's where you can describe the type of partner and partnership relationship you are seeking to develop. Will a contractual relationship suffice, or are you proposing to join with another company and form a completely separate entity? The exact nature of the partnership relationship will usually depend on the specific companies involved. But for now, you should offer management an idea of the working partnership. For example:

> *Facility Managers purchase maintenance services today from a multitude of service providers. We propose to provide a convenient, single source for several types of facility services, including: custodial, HVAC, grounds keeping, pest control, roof maintenance and more. Our service will provide consolidated purchasing and invoicing. We will provide these services through a joint venture with several other best-in-class service providers. The partnership will be marketed and sold under its own brand identity. Service providers will invoice the new venture at preferred pricing levels, with a small percentage retained by the joint venture for marketing and other overhead costs. Service providers will hold equity stakes in the joint venture, the size of which will depend on the specific services provided, and the expected levels of participation of each provider.*

Also included in this section should be an update of the development work completed to date. Where or how was the idea generated? Have there been any discussions with potential partners to date? With customers?

Market Analysis

Make sure you address each of the following:

A. **Industry Trends** – How has customer need evolved? What forces influence the market? What is the expected market growth rate? Are there substitute products? How is this need being met today?

B. **Target Markets** – Rank segments by industry, geography, size, etc. and list reasons for segment relative attractiveness. What are the expected growth rates for target segments? Why are these segments being targeted?

C. **Value Proposition** – How does your product/service meet the defined need(s) within the defined target segments? What are the advantages of your product/service over alternatives? Why will customers buy from you?

D. **SWOT Analysis** – Define the strengths, weaknesses, opportunities and threats of your offering relative to the competition. Include alternative methods that customer needs can be met.

E. **Relationship to Existing Line of Products/Services** – How does this new product/service fit within your existing line? Are you cannibalizing existing products/services? What impact will it have on your overall product/service offering?

F. **Additional Research** – What additional research is required? Describe proposed research projects with budget estimates.

Marketing Plan

A. **Distribution Channels** – How do you plan to take your product/service to market? What sales and marketing channels will be used? How will these channels be compensated?

B. **Pricing Strategy** – Define your proposed pricing structure. How does this compare to the competition? Where will your product/service be positioned on the competitive pricing scale?

C. **Product Positioning** – How will your product/service be positioned relative to competitive offerings in terms of other product/service attributes (quality, timeliness, durability, customer service, etc.)?

D. **Communications Strategy** – What is your main message to the target segments? How will it be communicated? What is the expected communications budget?

Operations Plan

A. **Start-up Activities** – What has transpired to this point? How will the partnership be supported organizationally? What types of infrastructure changes are required? What needs to occur before the product/service can be delivered?

B. **Day-to-Day Operations** – Walk-thru expected sales cycle and product/service delivery cycle.

C. **Staffing** – What are current and expected staffing levels? What type of organization will be needed to support the partnership? Include a projected organization chart.

D. **Oversight** – A small committee that includes at least one member of senior management from both partnering organizations. The oversight committee should meet at least once a quarter and monitor progress of the partnership towards its business goals. It can also help to resolve large-scale problems quickly.

E. **Training** – What types of training for employees will be required? Include budget estimates.

Financial Analysis & Attachments

A. Economics & Assumptions – Define expected gross margins and cash flows. Show evidence/research that market will support projected pricing levels.

B. Partnership vs. Alternatives – Show a cost/risk comparison of a strategic partnership vs. internal development vs. acquisition. Why is partnering preferred over the alternatives?

C. Start-up Costs – Budget immediate capital needs and on-going operating costs. Don't try to low-ball these costs. The credibility of the partnering team and management support for the partnership itself will erode quickly if costs extend well beyond budget.

D. Risk Assessment – Define major risks, including possible competitive reactions. What are plans for mitigating these risks?

E. Supporting Schedules – Cash flow statements, balance sheets, etc.

F. Market Studies – Publications, reports, articles, etc. to support statements concerning market/industry trends.

Now the Real Fun Begins

Ok. You've got a draft of your plan together. Notice the use of the word "draft." Now it's time to sell it to your organization. Hopefully, throughout the planning process, and even before it began, the partnership vision has been shared with upper management. So when your plan hits their desks requesting their comments, they won't write back, *What the hell is this?*

Usually the best way to get buy-in is to send your plan to key managers you need to win over, give them a few days to digest it, and then convene a meeting at which they can express any concerns they have. Your executive sponsor can help grease the skids and prepare management to review the plan. At the plan review meeting(s) you'll need to have your radar ready and well-tuned. Listen carefully to the concerns of all involved. Identify whether the concerns are with the details of the plan (schedule, budget, process, etc.) or with the concept itself. Budget and other details can be worked out, but if you hear questions like: *Why are we really doing this? Are these worthwhile objectives? Why do we need a partner anyway?*, these indicate someone who needs convincing that you've done a thorough analysis and are convinced, along with many others, that partnering is the best way to achieve the stated objectives, and that the objectives themselves are well-qualified.

And don't be the only one who carries the partnering torch forward within your company. Use a sponsor from senior management to take your message to non-believing executives. Review the financials and assumptions with them to try to pinpoint their discomfort. Address their concerns with an open mind – after all, they have extensive industry knowledge and may have hit upon something you missed in your analysis.

Be willing to negotiate within the context of the plan. You don't need to fall on your sword over every issue. Choose your battles carefully. If it's an issue that you feel is absolutely critical to overall success, be prepared to fight for it – not literally (unless you're sure you can take the guy), but have your support documentation ready to explain exactly why something needs to be done the way you've defined it in your plan. And save your fights for the big issues. Don't waste your energy and reputation fighting over smaller details at this early stage in the project. Remember: it's a plan, not a spouse. You're not married to it. The important thing is that you have a plan from which to base ensuing discussions and gain buy-in from key stakeholders.

United Support

The Partnership Plan helps you gain a foothold within upper management to sell the partnering concept and gain the approvals and budget dollars necessary to begin the actual partnering process. Remember to use sponsors. If you're able to effectively make your case, strong leadership will spread the message that the company is going ahead with this endeavor, and even if someone does not agree with it, <u>everyone</u> needs to give it their full support for it to be successful.

This is a very key juncture of the entire Partnering with a Purpose process (try to say that 5 times fast). The venture is now beyond an idea. It should be a well-defined concept with a detailed plan and estimates backed by sound analysis. The plan is the point-of-sale tool your team needs to make its case internally. Some level of buy-in needs to be achieved with every key resource (resource = person for us non-enlightened) within your organization. Your company simply should not continue on into the development phase of the partnering process without obtaining across-the-board support. And I don't mean everyone needs to be turned into a cheerleader, although that'd be very interesting. They just need to show full support, be it in resources or leadership, to the process going forward. This is where upper management needs to step up to the plate and make the decision. Opponents need to speak now or hold their peace, and their tongues. Specific details will be worked out later, but if someone's opposed to the entire concept, let them stand and be heard now. Take the time here to address people's fundamental concerns, because when this train leaves the station, everyone better be on board.

Now Let's Go Partner

So with management buy-in to your plan, you're now ready to get off the wall and join the party. The music's hot and your feet are tapping.

If you're like me, you've got a couple drinks in you for courage. So let's get out on that dance floor and show everyone what we've got!

Aw, #%&*!! We need someone to dance with!!

Chapter 4 – Will You Be My Partner?

"The meeting of two personalities is like the contact of two chemical substances: if there is any reaction, both are transformed."

Carl Jung

Here we go talking about human nature again. Sorry, I just can't help myself. So many aspects of strategic partnering, for both good and ill, are reflective of, and even dependent upon, some basic characteristics of human interaction. Some of these implications have already been mentioned: the need for multi-layered communication, obtaining buy-in from would-be naysayers and having no hidden agendas to name a few. But this application of human behavioral traits to partnering really becomes relevant when discussing attracting and evaluating companies as potential partners.

So far you've taken a close look at your own company – uncovered all the blemishes, pimples and rashes in the clear light of day. But like I said before, your company is no different than any other group of human beings – there are flaws, to be sure, but there are also many strengths and core competencies within your business that few, if any, organizations can match. You need to be confident in the strengths of your company in order to attract the best qualified partner prospects.

Looking for that Special Someone

Looking for a partner means giving up your business bachelorhood and find the perfect business – that one in a million company that accepts your organization for what it really is – blemishes and all. A partner that will make the future look brighter, the coffee taste better, and your annual report a lot more enjoyable to read. But where do you go to look for this soul mate of strategy to begin the courtship ritual? Well, you could try something like this:

Single Business Seeks Same

Growing company seeks creative, open-minded business for LTR; must enjoy increased revenues, improved value propositions and walks on the beach.

Serious replies only.

Let's share our common goals!!

Besides sounding desperate, this type of approach will not generate the qualified list you're looking for, and you spend way too much time and resources analyzing businesses that are poor fits for your company.

Businesses, just like individuals, naturally look for traits and competencies that complement their own. Just like a woman and a man bring different strengths and weaknesses into a marriage, two businesses can bring their own unique competencies into a strategic alliance. And in both cases, if the fit is right, not only are strong unions formed, but each party is also made stronger by the alliance.

For example, when I was single I used to be absolutely terrible at managing my checking account. I would never bother to balance my checkbook and would end up bouncing checks left and right. But since I've been married, this problem has disappeared. My wife Carol, who is very organized, manages our account and makes sure we balance every month. A perfect solution, right? Ok, she won't let me anywhere near the checkbook, but the point is, it's no longer a problem for us because we both recognize she's the best one for this job. And if you ask her, we're still looking for the jobs that I can do well.

Narrowing the Field

So how do we go about finding potential partners? I think it's difficult (but not impossible) to enter into any type of alliance with a company where there's no pre-existing relationship whatsoever. If you think about it, most of the relationships we have in our own lives start out as casual acquaintances. Except for the rare instance, we usually get to know people through some shared interest (work, ski club, yodeling class, monster truck rallies, etc.) This can also be said of B2B alliances. Your best sources for partner prospects are the existing relationships your company has with customers, vendors, competitors, trade organizations and anywhere else businesspeople interact. Someone on your management team may even have a personal relationship with a potential partner.

But before you start asking around your organization for contacts, review your Partnership Plan for the details concerning the type of partner that best fits your strategic business model. From your plan, you should be able to generate a broad brush profile of your "dream partner." You should be able to define, at least in general terms, the following:

- Type of business you'd like to partner with

- Complementary capabilities (intellectual capital, development, delivery, etc.)

- Reputation in the marketplace

- Commercial/Industrial markets served

- Geographical markets served

- Relative size of the business.

This is a good starting point, and it should be sufficient to generate a list of 5-10 partner candidates.

After you have a starting candidate list together, now we need to put on our marketing hats and consider the following question:

Now we all know that your company is the absolute best, despite any flaws we've identified. We understand that it's the greatest place in the world to work, or else why would an intelligent, business-savvy, rising star like you work there in the first place, right? This, however, does not mean that you don't need to do *some* selling to partner prospect companies in order to generate interest.

Before you approach any of your target prospects, you need to package the partnering opportunity in a way that you, or someone else in your organization, can easily present. This may be nothing more than a single-page document or a 3-6 slide presentation (we're not trying to create more work here; upper management needs no help doing that!). But at a minimum, your "partner package" should address the following:

- High-level strategy driving your company's need to partner (e.g., "We're looking to increase customer satisfaction and retention by expanding the service packages our customers can purchase along with our products.")

- The type of partner you're looking for (products, markets served, etc.)

- Why you're specifically interested in them as a partner?

- What's in it for the partner company?

- What's in it for your own company.?

All of what's listed above should be readily available from within your Partnership Plan. Note that at this stage we're not providing too many details…those will come later, and only after a non-disclosure agreement has been signed. But for now, we're giving select prospects just a little taste of the tremendous growth opportunity that a partnership with your company offers.

Flowers, Candy and the NDA

Your preparations to go out and pitch your vision to would-be partners should include having a non-disclosure agreement ready should prospects show interest and both parties want to proceed to the next step in the process. It's natural for businesses to want to hold their cards close to the vest, and NDA's can serve to provide a measure of security as the two companies get to know one another. They can help minimize the nervous twitches of executive types, and open the door to allow the sharing of strategic information.

As strategic alliances of all shapes, sizes and flavors have become more popular, there has been a proliferation of NDA templates flying around B2B cyberspace. I'm not going to go into great details about how to construct an NDA. Use this acid test to determine if your template will work: *Does the NDA allow for the exchange of confidential information?* If the answer is "No" then your NDA needs work.

Let me just take a moment here to wave my red flag…there, that felt good. But seriously folks, here's a potentially big barrier we first mentioned in Chapter 2. If participants are unable or unwilling to share strategic information, there's little or no hope of developing a successful strategic alliance. The NDA must serve to lower the hackles of all involved and allow companies to REALLY get to know one another. How else can either party make an informed decision of whether or not to move forward with the partnership?

Your Boardroom or Mine?

OK, you've got your sales pitch, your NDA, and a list of 5–10 partner candidates. Finally, you're ready to start approaching businesses about becoming partners. Again, look internally for any existing relationships with your prospect list. Start at the very top of your own organization when identifying these relationships. Initiating the partnering discussions at the "C" level will move things along much more rapidly than if you tried starting at mid-management and working your way up through both organizations.

Where possible, use your "C" level to initiate the contact. Make sure you arm him/her with your sales pitch materials. Trade shows and other industry forums provide excellent opportunities to discreetly approach prospects with your idea. But don't show your hand too quickly. The initial goal is to merely indicate that you're interested in discussing the possibility of some type of collaborative relationship between your two organizations, and that you'd like to have a meeting to discuss it further. If the two "C's" agree, then it's just a matter of scheduling and identifying who needs to attend the meeting.

In preparation for the meeting, send your NDA template to the prospect to get the legal ball rolling. Keep the number of meeting participants to a minimum. At this point, we're just looking to lay out our vision and gauge mutual interest - the fewer people who know that your company is looking to partner with X in order to do Y, the better. Take the approach with the prospect that this is to be a semi-formal discussion, and in order to share some of your strategic vision with them, you need to have a signed NDA in place.

The First Date

Shine your shoes, comb your hair, and for heaven's sake, don't wear that ugly tie! As they say, you've only got one chance to make a first impression, so don't blow it. The initial meeting you have with a prospect moves the discussion from the casual into the formal arena. Sending your NDA template to them ahead of time and specifying key players from both organizations to attend sends the message: *Hey! This is not going to be just a social call. We're coming for some serious discussion and would like you to be prepared for the same.*

It's important, if at all possible, to have your executive sponsor with you on this first meeting. Preferably it's the same person who owns the pre-existing relationship with the prospect company. This puts the meeting on a friendly basis from the get-go, and should help the information sharing process.

Since you requested this meeting, it's appropriate that you control the meeting agenda. The objectives for the meeting, which you should send ahead of time, along with your NDA, should be pretty simple. Something along the lines of:

- To present an overview of your partnership vision

- To gauge interest from the prospect

- To plan next steps.

The first part, presenting your company's partnership vision, should be easy by this point. You've got your partnership marketing bundle, extracted from the Partnership Plan, at the ready. Take special care not to provide too many details to the prospect – remember, even with an NDA in place, this is still an external audience. The details of the partnership relationship should be left to the Terms & Conditions of the Partnership Agreement. But before we can get to that step, both parties need to carefully evaluate and decide whether or not to enter into formal partnering discussions. Your goal with this initial presentation is to communicate a sound, well-thought-out strategy, and to explain their role in the partnership. And don't forget to wow them with your professionalism. This first impression you make goes a long way towards convincing prospects that yours is a company with which they should seriously consider being aligned.

When you've finished laying out your partnership vision, shut up and listen. Gauge first reactions - positive, negative, lukewarm… whatever. Take note of their levels of enthusiasm towards the proposed alliance. If your prospects don't seem very talkative at this point (perhaps they're just stunned by your professionalism), here's a few conversation starters:

- So, what's your overall impression?

- Are there any parts that just don't make sense?

- Do you think our estimates are overly optimistic?

- Do you currently use strategic alliances? If so, what types of results have you seen?

- How does this proposal fit within your growth strategy?

- What's your assessment of the synergies that would be created by the partnership?

- Any concerns you see from a 40,000-foot level? Channel conflicts? Legal issues?

- Does your company have memberships at any really nice country clubs?

Not much guidance I can provide here for determining exactly how much interest the prospect has in your partnership proposal. If they sit there stone-faced and say nothing, or if they say something on the order of, "We just don't see partnering on our *horizon* (radar screen, plate, wish list, etc.)," chances are they're not real interested. If you meet this type of resistance, and they're one of your top prospects, you might suggest a less-integrated form of partnership, such as a limited campaign where sales and/or marketing channels are shared and finder's fees are included. But hopefully, you'll get a response that's at least *cautiously optimistic*, which means, "I may be interested, but need to learn more."

To conclude the meeting, mention that you are still in the evaluation stage and are considering one or more partnering alternatives. If the prospect shows interest, let them know that as part of the evaluation process, you will need to gather some more detailed information about them to ensure you have the best match possible. As a next step, suggest that you'd like to send them a summary of your discussion, including their expressed concerns, and a list of information that you'd like to share between your two organizations to move to the evaluation stage. Then, you'll probably need to schedule a subsequent meeting to which both parties could bring specified information to discuss and/or exchange.

So, your first date then comes to an end - you kiss at the door and go home. Not too exciting, right? But remember, your objective here is to simply present your case, gauge interest and let them know there's more to come…a lot more.

Repeat the process with the other companies on your prospect list. For each one, make sure you go into the meeting with a completely open mind. Businesses that, at first glance, may not seem to be a good fit for you can often, upon further investigation, turn out to be exactly the type of partner you need to make the venture successful.

Partner Evaluation

This "first date" process should serve to condense your prospect list down to 2 or 3 top candidates. Even if one of your prospects appears to be head and shoulders above the rest, you should still move at least 2-3 into the formal evaluation stage. And don't automatically put a prospect on the top of your list just because they've exhibited the most enthusiasm for the partnership out of the gate. They may be the company on your list with the most to hide, and are desperate for an alliance in order to patch gaping holes within their own organization.

Now it's time to take out your magnifying glass and carefully examine each of your finalists. You should have forewarned all of them during your first dates that you would be asking for some more detailed information. Your goal here is to establish a framework to compare and contrast your finalists over several key criteria. And while the specific information needed to complete this comparison will vary over partnering scenarios, you should be able to construct a comparison chart on your prospects that looks something like this:

Partner Evaluation Criteria	Weight (1-4)	Thongs Are Us		Thong World		Everything Thong	
		Score (1-10)	Wgtd. Score	Score (1-10)	Wgtd. Score	Score (1-10)	Wgtd. Score
Financially Stable	4	7	28	9	36	6.5	26
Partnership Would Create a Compelling Value Proposition	3	6.5	19.5	10	30	9	27
Quality Reputation	3	8	24	7	21	10	30
Strategic Business Fit	4	9	36	8.5	34	7	28
Market Coverage	2	5	10	7	14	10	20
Sr. Management Commitment	4	7.5	32	6	24	8.5	34
Viable Growth Opportunity for Both Parties	4	7	28	8	32	8	32
TOTALS		50	177.5	55.5	191	59	197

I believe in using weighted criteria; it allows you to include many more company attributes in your evaluation. And while all of these attributes may not be crucial for success, you still need to consider them in your partner selection process. The weights will vary depending on the type of partnership you're looking to develop. For example, in a sales/marketing channel alliance, with short-term goals and a well-defined fee and commission structure, Market Coverage would probably take on more importance vs. Financial Stability. If you're aligning with a company to service your products, Quality Reputation should receive the most weight.

Time to get out my little red flag again. Make sure you take the time to work through this evaluation process carefully. Your goal is to identify the prospect that provides the best strategic fit for your company and the partnership model you've developed. Be both diligent and patient with companies while gathering information. Even with an NDA, there's still quite a bit of red tape most businesses need to cut through in order to get information released. Believe me, the time you spend here will return many times over because it maximizes your chances of selecting the right partner.

Your due diligence should include tapping these sources for information:

- Annual reports
- Revenue breakdowns by product, historic trends
- Patents
- Lists of major customers
- Local chambers of commerce
- 10k reports
- Major competitors

- Executive biographies
- Organizational structure, and any recent restructure
- Dun & Bradstreet reports
- BBB
- Trade associations (e.g., industry forums, SAMA [Strategic Account Management Association], trade shows, etc.)

A list of major customers provides especially good insight into whether the prospect is pursuing, and winning, the same types of customers as your company. And if you have any customers in common, these customers will give you tremendous insight into how the prospect performs...whether they're really as good as they look on paper.

All of the information sources listed above are good, but the best insight you're going to get from the prospect will come from the people who work there. This is a good way to get all the news that's unfit to print. Doesn't mean it's bad - it's just that editorial comments from people on the inside can tell us much more than any publication can. Tap any relationship that exists with your partner prospects to find out what the working atmosphere is like, general employee morale, any recent organizational restructuring, prevailing attitudes towards partnering, divisions of responsibility, etc. All of these sources need to figure into your partner decision process.

And don't forget about the country club memberships.

One Potato, Two Potato...

If, after all your analysis, you're faced with a tough choice between two or more attractive prospects that both scored very well on your evaluation, GOOD! This means you have alternatives, and a back-up, in case the partnership does not perform to expectations (highly unlikely because you'll be so well prepared after reading this book). If there is one and only one prospect that clearly stands out above the rest, this is also a good scenario, just not as optimal as the first. The good news is you have a well-qualified partner prospect, the bad news is your choices are limited, which in turn reduces your negotiating leverage.

But Uncle Dave, what if we're not comfortable with _any_ of the alternatives?

In this case, you need to go back and review your Partnership Plan. In light of your plan, ask yourself:

- Were our partner expectations too high?

- Did we eliminate any prospects early in the process for valid reasons? Can these be re-visited?

- Was our prospect list too small to begin with? Can it be expanded?

- Was our evaluation criteria too limiting?

- Were the evaluations we gave our prospects based on fact or opinion?

- INTERNALLY, ARE WE SOLD ON THE CONCEPT OF PARTNERING AT ALL?

With your brilliant insight you'll no doubt infer that this last question may be the most critical, especially if, after going through this process several times, you still find yourselves with no acceptable partnering alternatives. If this is the case, count your blessings that you've been able to discover that partnering does NOT fit your business model at this early stage of the game, rather than finding out later after you make a sizeable investment in a failing venture.

But with well-qualified alternatives, you should be able to make a sound partnering recommendation to your executive sponsor, then the rest of your senior management team. This recommendation should be accompanied with your analysis of all the data you've collected over the past several weeks. This analysis should convince all concerned that you've done your homework and have arrived at the best possible solution.

The solution now needs to be "sold" internally. Again, don't skimp on this step. Process owners and key management personnel in your company need to fully understand the process that drove your team to the partner choice it did. For certain, there will be some who would have preferred a different choice. So, to prevent the negativity later when things don't go quite according to plan (Can't you just hear it? "You know, I never did like <u>them</u> as a partner choice."), you need to get everyone on board before you hoist anchor.

The Partnership Agreement

Are you a real cutthroat negotiator? Do you pride yourself on walking out of the auto dealership leaving the poor sales slob in such a state of disarray that he's ready to try a different occupation? Well, you might want to check your primal negotiating instincts at the door for this one. That's because the goal with any strategic alliance model is to create a true WIN-WIN scenario.

Note that it's WIN-WIN, not WIN-win that we're going for here. If your model does not allow your partner to prosper and share in the fundamental success of the alliance, then it will look more like a vendor-customer relationship. Such a model differs from a strategic alliance in that control is very much tilted towards one side, and there is no investment in mutual success. To reap the many benefits of strategic partnering, your model must align with the strategic objectives of both organizations.

Sample Partnership Model

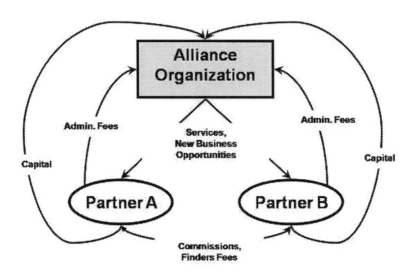

Whatever model and agreement you put in front of your partner prospect, know that they will immediately ask themselves questions like:

- What's in it for me?

- What risks are there with this model?

- What's in it for me?

- What type of investments (capital, people, etc.) are required?

- What's in it for me?

- Are fees, commission, etc. fairly distributed among partners?

- What's in it for me?

- How will this impact my existing operations?

- What's in it for me?

So to the extent that you can make the answers to these questions readily available in your partner model and alliance agreement, the easier it will be for your prospect to comprehend and make a final decision. They must be able to plainly see not only your partnership vision, but also how this vision matches to their own growth strategy.

As with the NDA, there are many existing templates for partnership agreements. But here are a few guidelines. At a minimum, your partnership agreement should:

- Define the purpose of the alliance

- Provide a means for either party to terminate the agreement with reasonable notice

- Define the partnership-specific organizational support structure

- Define up-front investments required from both partners

- Define any oversight structure or procedure for strategic direction and conflict resolution

- Identify any on-going fee structure

- Define the terms of payment for the above

- Contain the terms & conditions necessary to calm the fears of both partners' legal teams.

And remember to keep the KISS (Keep It Simple, Stupid) mentality in mind when developing this agreement. The more complicated things look, the more reluctance you're going to face from both your partner prospect and within your own company.

So now we have our model, as defined within our Partnership Plan, with all the gory details of exactly how this Frankenstein of ours is going to work. We have our signed NDA and our Partnership Agreement. We have buy-in from all the key players on our own side of the fence.

Sounds like we're ready to pop the question.

The Proposal

Afraid of commitment? Well, then perhaps partnerships aren't for you. Because now we've come to the part where we have to decide who's going to be our traveling partner on this road to strategic alliance paradise.

Up to now, we've pretty much kept things loose and informal. Yes, we elevated the process to "serious" when we started going through each other's financial reports, but now we're about to put forth a formal business alliance proposal to our chosen prospect. The time for loafers and flats is over ladies and gentlemen – it's wingtips and heels time!

I recommend a formal approach to delivering and signing the Partnership Agreement, mainly because we're all about results. This book is called *Partnering with a Purpose*, not *Partnering for Fun & Recreation* (although that sounds like a good read, too). We want our partner to understand right from the outset that this is a serious business venture that's going to take significant investments of time, talent and other capital in order to be successful. So we need to send a strong signal that this is not something they should enter into lightly.

After delivering your formal request and Partnership Agreement, be patient but persistent. There will probably be several legal salvos fired back and forth before both parties come to agreement. You may even have to do more internal selling when certain people get upset with the process ("What the $%#@* is taking so long?!"). The key for all is to keep the end goal(s) in mind. Risk mitigation will no doubt be on everyone's mind. But if you end up taking <u>all</u> the risk out of the project, you've also most likely taken away the reward opportunities as well.

It's important to give your future partner the time and security they need to make their decision so they can enter into the partnership with high expectations and great enthusiasm. And if by chance no agreement can be reached, even on a short-term and less strategic basis, then just shake hands and repeat the process with your next best prospect. After all, there's usually more than just one path to the top of a mountain.

"I Now Pronounce You Partner and Partner"

You've got the deal signed. Give yourself a pat on the back. Have a drink (or two, you certainly deserve it). You've taken the partnering concept from the clouds to the pavement. You've been through an evaluation of your own business in an attempt to identify possible obstacles to implementing a successful partner model. You've defined a model that fits your company's strategic growth initiatives and gained buy-in from key shareholders. You've gone through an exhaustive partner prospect evaluation process in order to identify the very best partner choice. You've been through round after round of legal wrangling over the Partnership Agreement, and have finally produced a document that's agreeable to both sides. Great job!

Now, I don't want to be the one to rain on your parade, but…

The good news is: You now have a strong framework for strategic growth.

The bad news is: Now the <u>real work</u> begins.

If you want another drink now, I'll completely understand.

Chapter 5 – "And They're Off!"

Now, let's take our new partnership and go make some money!

Huh? What's that you say?

Dave, shouldn't we crawl before we walk? Walk before we run? Aren't you being rather short-sighted, tactical vs. strategic, and only concerned with near-term returns?

You bet your assets I am!! And for good reason, too!

We've worked very hard to this point to get our partnership off the ground and headed towards meeting and exceeding well-defined business objectives. We've managed to gain buy-in from key stakeholders, and freed up most of the resources we need to make this thing take off. Basically, we've persuaded those holding the purse-strings to say *OK, we're willing to give this a try*. We've bought ourselves a bit of time to prove that our partnering concept really works, but that's about it. The door's been opened for us, but it could start to close very fast on us, if we don't start 'walking the talk'.

The time to deliver is now.

We need to prove that our partnership model works in the real world of dollars, ROI's, bottom lines and *please-don't-call-me-anymore's*.

53

The Start-Up Model

So exactly how do we go about making the most of this well crafted opportunity? I recommend that all employees involved in the partnership – from the president right down to the lowly consultant (a.k.a., that overpaid, sub-human life form that thinks he knows all there is to know about your business) – should consider the partnership as a brand new start-up company. This perspective will help guide your actions during those first crucial months of the partnership.

Ideally, any new business would like to have all the time and resources needed to get every detail of their enterprise, right down to the company stationery, in place before going to the market and actually trying to generate sales. For most entrepreneurs, however, there's a pretty small time window you have available to generate a positive cash flow before your tiny well of start-up capital runs dry and you get added to that ever-growing publication: *Fabulous Business Ideas That Never Got Off the Ground*. You should view your newly-formed partnership exactly the same way. We have a very finite amount of time and resources to prove out our business case and to generate some traction. We need to focus on the big picture – namely, securing customers and locking in revenue streams by aggressively pursuing any and all logical business opportunities. The customized pens and coffee mugs can come later, after we can pay for them with our self-generated cash flow.

To this end, your goal at the outset should be to instill the partnership with a real entrepreneurial spirit – that everyone involved with the partnership project are on the ground floor of something special that could grow into a huge success and make everyone rich and famous (Me? I'd settle for rich). All of us want to have our names attached to successful ventures. You need people with this type of enthusiasm going the extra mile to make sure the partnership gets off the ground. Our collective 'attention to detail' has never been so important.

Not that you need to start the partnership operations from a garage, using the library to make copies, having frozen pizza for your corporate luncheons, and so on. But it certainly helps if you can fill your partnership staff positions with people who have that type of go the extra mile mindset – the type who don't mind humble beginnings if there's the promise of a bright future out there for them. So it's important that the start-up mentality gets communicated from the top and permeated throughout both partner organizations, to the point where bright, ambitious people are virtually lining up to be part of this tremendous growth opportunity. Your team's aggressiveness here at the outset is critical to success. Everyone needs to be both highly focused, highly motivated and above all, not standing on the sidelines waiting for something to happen before they decide to jump into the game.

If yours is like most new business ventures, at the outset your organization chart will look something like this:

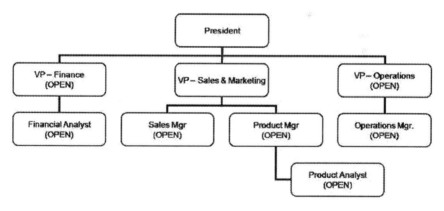

And if you don't already have at least one client under contract, people will say that, even in this infantile state, your organization is overstaffed, which is probably true. In order to justify adding more people, there needs to be some clearly defined, imminent revenue opportunities – in the form of signed proposals, contracts, purchase orders...whatever – we just need clear justification to be able to get the right people on board and fully engaged.

But Dave, what if I can't get approval to hire anyone?

Don't panic. You're just experiencing the "try before you buy" syndrome that engulfs senior managers of all types everywhere when faced with one too many unknowns. They're signaling that they want to move cautiously before jumping into something that has the potential to blow their legs off. The only cure is to bring in new business quickly – solid revenue opportunities – that will give all concerned parties sufficient reason to get behind the alliance. We all enjoy being part of a success.

The key is to focus all partnership activity, from whatever resources you can steal, on immediate sales and profitability. Sales feeds the beast, as they say, and as long as you have paying customers, you can make a case for expanding the partnership organization. Revenue-generating business requires a support structure; non-revenue activity does not.

So exactly how do we go about landing that first big deal?

"Congratulations – It's a Value Proposition!"

You've formed this partnership with the goal of bringing something very real to the market place: new products with more benefits, new service bundles, greater efficiencies – you name it. The point is you have created a great story to tell – a value proposition, to answer that initial qualifying question in the prospect's mind: *Why should I be talking to these people?*

Great question. One all your employees with customer contact need to be ready to answer. In fact, all of your marketing materials, from point-of-sale to media ads to direct mail, should be focused on the value your alliance creates and ultimately delivers for the customer. And the simpler you can make your message, the better the retention will be within your prospects (didn't know you'd be getting some sage marketing advice on top of the partnering wisdom, did you?).

So don't skimp on the initial marketing materials. Get a professional-looking piece that helps you deliver your value proposition right between the eyes of your target market. If you've done your homework to this point, the value of your alliance will jump off the page. Your prospects will readily understand what it is your alliance brings to the market place. They will feel fortunate to be one of the first to take advantage of your new offering.

Ideally, both partner companies have been "talking up" the partnership to current customers as the details of the new alliance have been worked out. By the partnership start-up date, these opportunities should be identified, cultivated, and well into the sales cycle. Close them – FAST! Even if it's for a very limited, near-term engagement, we need to prime the revenue pump. So in the partnership's infancy, it's critical that communications to any external audiences are tightly controlled to ensure that no one is out there making promises that can't be met.

Now - Prepare for Success

Your plan for the structure and growth of the partnership is one thing – planning on actually delivering the product/service to the customer is quite another. The easiest way to torpedo the entire alliance is to fall short of product/service delivery promises. The entire team needs to be confident that it can deliver on the promise that's being sold to prospects.

When and where economically practical, it's a good idea to run through some internal or external pilots or beta tests of the concept to ensure that all of your service/product delivery mechanisms – sales, IT, operations, billing, etc. – are in place and fully capable of entering and processing orders to full completion. Small bumps are to be expected, but any landmines which are laying in wait need to be triggered, identified and properly defused before the real deal begins. Just like a racehorse, if we stumble on our first step out of the starting gate, it puts us behind and makes it even more difficult to win the race.

No doubt the naysayers will be looking closely over your shoulder as you roll out the new venture, just waiting for early failures so they can point their bony little cynical fingers at you and say *I told you so.* Don't give them the opportunity! Button down your order fulfillment and operational process with all your i's dotted and t's crossed. Baby-sit your first few transactions through the process, making sure that all commitments are met with time to spare. Then follow up, follow up and follow up some more!

In the start-up phase, an alliance has no specific track record to speak of. You must therefore rely on the histories and reputations of the two partner organizations to support the promise inherent within the value proposition. But there will be skepticism nonetheless, and be prepared to hear it early and often. More than price, your prospects' biggest concerns will be: *Can these guys really deliver as promised? What are the consequences of a product/service failure? How's my fantasy football team doing?*

You've probably heard the saying; *No one ever lost their job purchasing from IBM.* This aphorism speaks to the importance of product/service delivery, reliability and support. These critical components of your overall offering comprise the risk in the customers' eyes of doing business with you. The mission of your sales force, and your entire organization for that matter, is to assuage these concerns from your prospects. With a reliable delivery process in place, your message can be delivered to prospects with utmost confidence, and your sales reps won't have to be telling clients, *Well, I can't promise you anything, but… don't we have a cool brochure?*

The Trophy Account

Your initial opportunities will serve two main needs of the fledgling partnership: 1. Cash generation (always my personal favorite), and 2. Track record or trophy accounts. These are the key customers that you can use as references in both your conversations with prospects, as well as your collateral materials. These accounts can confirm to your prospects that your value proposition is more than marketing spin – that you really can deliver the goods as promised.

The more well-known your trophy accounts are the better. Did you ever see a movie review in the newspaper that looked something like this?

"…I laughed so hard, my dentures fell out!"

Sam "Spittoon" Weaver
Corn Cob County Chronicle

Upon reading a review like this, your first thought tends to be, *What? Couldn't they get a more prominent publication to give this thing a decent review?* Either that, or *Exactly how did he earn a nickname like "Spittoon"?*

In any event, you'll naturally conclude that if they could have received a positive endorsement from a better known source, they absolutely would have. It's a good bet the movie studio didn't get a great review from USA Today or the New York Times and then decide not to use it in their movie ad in favor of the quote from the Corn Cob County Chronicle.

So try to obtain a trophy account with a name that's going to have significant meaning to your prospects. And, as mentioned before, it's important that your initial reviews be glowing, yet honest and accurate.

"This venture is amazing. I laughed, I cried. It became part of me!"

Ok, that may be a bit much. Here's basically all you need:

"They delivered the value as promised. I was very pleased with the results"

Now you've added some credibility to your message.

To gain a trophy account, you'll no doubt need to leverage some existing relationships. To get in the door, to get a meeting with the decision makers, to get that first pilot program – I don't want to turn this into a sales guide, but all of these important steps will require both partner organizations to utilize their established professional trust and call on the most tenured relationships in their respective portfolios.

Reality Check

If anywhere within these pages I've made the initial sales process sound easy, it's completely unintentional. In past lives, as a sales consultant and strategic account manager, I've "carried a bag" with all the quotas and threats of slow dismemberment that accompany most sales positions. In short, I know how difficult it can be to land new business, especially with a brand new product or service.

No doubt closing these initial sales opportunities will be a huge effort - one that both partner organizations will need to get behind and push with all their collective might. In previous chapters we've discussed getting everyone, within both partner organizations, rowing in the same direction, singing out of the same hymnal, marching to the same drummer…insert whatever overused phrase you'd like. The point is that it's going to take two dedicated, fully supportive organizations to get this partnership plane off the ground.

I go back to my mantra of: *Communicate Communicate Communicate.* Get everyone involved. Let everyone know what the objectives are. The larger the team effort to land these first critical sales, the higher are the chances of success. So spread the word regarding your initial sales opportunities. See if others have ideas on how to close the deal. Who knows? Maybe someone from either partner company used to work there and can give a clear lay of the land.

Difficult? You bet. But that first taste of success is oh so sweet.

Toast Your Success

You mean it's time to celebrate? That I might actually get to enjoy part of this process? Gee, it's been such a party up to now.

Steady. When you land that first contract, yes you can absolutely celebrate. You and your team certainly deserve it. But make sure of two things first:

1. That your trophy accounts are delighted with the product/ service they've purchased, and the mechanisms are in place to keep them that way.

2. That any celebration includes your new partners. After all, they're in this with you, sink or swim.

So go ahead and pop the champagne corks. The partnership is up and running. We've got our first sales and the cash register has started to ring. Life is good.

What could possibly go wrong now?

Chapter 6 – Making Course Corrections

I'm sorry to say this
But sadly, it's true
That Bang-ups and Hang-ups can happen to you.

Dr. Seuss

Storms on the Horizon

Might as well face it now, your strategic alliance - with all the blood, sweat and tears you've poured into it - is going to stray off course. Something unexpected will undoubtedly happen and the question then is 'Are you and your team prepared to deal with the course correction?' There are just too many forces in the scary ocean of real-world business. Forget about keeping a straight and narrow course – just keeping that little boat of your strategic alliance afloat will be challenging enough. So what do we do when the stormy winds blow, the waves break over our bow, and our alliance starts taking on water?

First of all, consider this – if the partnership is not faced with some course corrections along the way, the chances are that your partnering model is not being sufficiently challenged, nor bringing optimal value to either partner organization. By their very nature, strategic alliances bring about change – new strategies, people, processes, infrastructure and systems. You can't push the envelope without expecting some level of pain. So keep pushing! But keep some aspirin (or other painkiller of choice) handy.

Secondly, take heart – our ship may be small, but she is strong. We've been diligent up to this point to put a sound plan together, get all key stakeholders on board, and validate the value we're bringing to the market. Now is the time for all that sweat equity (including some very fine groveling) to pay a return.

Don't Push the Panic Button

The next strategic alliance that has a smooth road to success will be the first. Expect there to be issues. Share that expectation throughout both partner organizations, and then no one should be surprised or disappointed when some problems do occur. Even the most detailed of plans rarely goes off without a hitch. Take this story from legendary Hollywood producer Cecil B. DeMille.

> *Cecil B. De Mille was making one of his great epic movies. He had six cameras at various points to pick up the overall action and five other cameras set up to film plot developments involving the major characters.*
>
> *"The large cast had begun rehearsing their scene at 6 a.m. They went through it four times and now it was late afternoon. The sun was setting and there was just enough light to get the shot done. De Mille looked over the panorama, saw that all was right, and gave the command for action.*

"One hundred extras charged up the hill; another hundred came storming down the same hill to do mock battle. In another location Roman centurions lashed and shouted at two hundred slaves who labored to move a huge stone monument toward its resting place. "Meanwhile the principal characters acted out, in close-up, their reactions to the battle on the hill. Their words were drowned out by the noise around them, but the dialogue was to be dubbed in later.*

"It took fifteen minutes to complete the scene. When it was over, De Mille yelled, 'Cut!' and turned to his assistant, all smiles. 'That was great!' he said.

"'It was, C.B.,' the assistant yelled back. 'It was fantastic! Everything went off perfectly!'

"Enormously pleased, De Mille turned to face the head of his camera crew to find out if all the cameras had picked up what they had been assigned to film. He waved to the camera crew supervisor.

"From the top of the hill, the camera supervisor waved back, raised his megaphone, and called out, 'Ready when you are, C.B.!'"

So What's Not Working?

Get out your shovels, because we're going digging for the truth. We need to carefully define any and all problems to identify root causes. Is the problem with sales & marketing, or more on the product/service delivery side of the coin? In any case, it's important not to scrap perfectly sound processes when the real issue lies elsewhere.

With many new strategic ventures, the problem might not be process or system related at all. It could be with some of the people involved.

As was mentioned earlier, a partnership in start-up mode challenges all its participants to break out of their traditional organizational roles and use new sets of muscles and ideas to get the job done. Some of the early employee selections might not be good fits for their particular assignments, or it could be that some of the people chosen to get your partnership off the ground are just not up to the challenge. This is certainly not an indictment of any individual. On the contrary, you need to have a bug somewhere in your personal operating system to even want to be part of a start-up. But new roles that were assigned as part of our start-up are probably not all going to be perfect fits. That's ok. Personnel change is inevitable. Don't be afraid of it. We have to put people in positions where they, and the partnership, can succeed. Reassignments can bring fresh eyes and enthusiasm to bear on our core issues.

Have no fear! Precisely identify and communicate the core problem that's slowing the success of the partnership. Don't try to throw sawdust on it like it was some steaming pile of consultants. Full disclosure will get us to a solution and back on track faster. Remember, we're dealing with a very small window of opportunity here and time is of the essence!

Share the Pain

Hopefully you were paying attention in Chapter 3, and an oversight committee has been established for the partnership. Now don't say, *What oversight committee?* The oversight committee consists of management, with at least one representative from senior management, from <u>both</u> partner organizations. Its purpose is to monitor the progress of the partnership AND resolve major issues.

So now is the time for the oversight committee to do more than just review financial results and make comments about marketing slogans (*Hmmm…that doesn't do much for me.*) Bring them together. Explain the problem and situation that you are encountering. And have a recommended solution ready to present, even if it might not be complete.

The goal with the oversight committee is to draw out their input and get their buy-in. After all, it's their partnership too. They should be able to "get down into the weeds" with you if that's what it takes to resolve issues or break down any barriers to success. Just because you've been a champion of the partnership to this point does not mean that you need to resolve any and all problems yourself. Others have already bought into the partnership and should be ready to step up and help when needed.

Listen to the Customer

Finding solutions to growth obstacles might not be as difficult as you think. The best place to start is with your customers. How do the partnership's problem(s) manifest themselves to customers? Also, ask your customers what issues, if any, they are experiencing. Do they see any ways in which the product or service can be improved? Defining the issue(s) to be solved in terms of end customer impact will help drive the implementation of a quick solution. Your initial keystone accounts carry quite a bit of clout with your senior management stakeholders. Let them help get the partnership back on course.

Surveys and focus groups are always good ways to gather customer feedback, but they can take a long time to get organized. A concise, well-written summary of a meeting with a large customer, with select customer quotes, can be circulated very quickly. It might be just what you need to move the partnership organization to act quickly.

All in the Same Boat

If we don't hang together, we shall hang separately

Benjamin Franklin, addressing American Revolutionaries

Getting back to the rocking boat example that began this chapter, a new partnership is usually rowing against some pretty strong currents. The sharks are circling and there's blood in the water. Now is not the time for in-fighting, name calling or insulting each other's wardrobe.

The partnership team members need to pull together and focus their collective efforts on identifying root causes, defining solutions and implementing them as quickly as possible. Finger pointing (especially the middle one) does nothing but slow down the process. Rogue behavior and splitter groups are inevitable, but keep everyone's eyes on the prize: an efficient partnership organization that's exceeding its financial and strategic objectives. Remember:

Shared Pain
+ Shared Solutions
Shared Success

Chapter 7 – Continuing Shared Success

When you build bridges you can keep crossing them.

Basketball coach Rick Pitino from his book <u>Lead to Success</u>

In the last chapter we addressed ways to handle problems with our newly formed partnership. Overcoming these problems quickly and efficiently will certainly help the partnership continue on the road to success, but did you know that success itself can also be a cause for a partnership to fail? More precisely, a failure to handle early success can drive even the most promising of partnerships straight to the morgue.

Sharing the Glory

We all know that success has many parents, but failure is an orphan. This certainly holds true for the early successes of a newly formed partnership. The same people who said *I told you so* when the inevitable start-up problems arose are now squeezing their fat, ego inflated heads into the photos of the partnership project team for the company newsletter.

Now, lesser individuals would be tempted to send scathing e-mails to the entire company exposing these cretins for the ever political, hypocritical desk jockeys they really are (gee, do you think I've crossed paths with a few?). But don't hit that Send button just yet. Take a cleansing breath, release all of that negative energy, and ask yourself, *Do I really need these people on the train if we're going to make it past the first station?* The most likely answer is yes, so stay your hand for the moment, and let's think about the future of the partnership – that is, unless you have a really good place to hide the bodies.

Since we're in this for the long haul, it makes sense to recognize anyone who played even a small role in getting the partnership off the ground. So now is not the time to be stingy with the accolades. Use any and all the modes of recognition your company has created - Employee-of-the-Month, Team Player, MVP, Impresario of Excellence, Grand Pubah of Projects, Maestro of Marketing – to give everyone on the team a great big warm and fuzzy. And for those awards that you receive yourself (see previous list), make sure you let everyone know it was truly a team effort. Don't worry about making a long acceptance speech. Chances are there's no orchestra that's going to cut you off so they can go to commercial.

I know I sound cynical (again) when discussing these company recognition programs, but this is actually important stuff. Just because we've achieved some modicum of success doesn't mean this journey is over; in fact, it is really just getting started. If we want our partnership to be a self-sustaining long-term enterprise, we're going to need all of the talented people we can get to know that there is something besides a paycheck in it for them. Both current and potential team members need to understand that someone is going to recognize the endless project meetings, the crisis-of-the-week dances, and the daily problem-solving shuffle that they do to keep things running smoothly. And even those seemingly worthless, backstabbing politicos mentioned above (yes, my therapy continues) need some love too. Because even if they don't make a worthwhile contribution to the team's success, at least they won't be laying landmines in your path. Just remember to keep tongue out of cheek and your lunch down when presenting them their awards. I never said this was going to be easy!

Where Does the Partnership Go From Here?

Success always provides more options than failure. We've talked about having well defined metrics in place to understand which direction the partnership is heading and how to make coarse corrections when and where necessary. Once some measure of success has been attained, however, it's a common mistake to keep the partner model static, believing that early growth will just continue on its own momentum.

The "if it ain't broke, don't fix it" business model doesn't seem to work any more. Even Super Bowl champions make changes in the off-season to adjust to the ever-changing competitive environment. At a minimum, the partnership will continue to require periodic business reviews – I recommend at least quarterly – to identify deficiencies and make corrections before small problems become big ones. The product, marketing and operations plans will need to evolve as well in order to adjust to ever-changing market conditions. Staffing plans will also require quarterly updates, not just because of turnover, but also due to new skill sets being required as the partnership, like any business, fights to keep up with, or preferably stay ahead of, the competition.

But you, being a smart (hey, you're reading this book, aren't you?), savvy predator in this particular business ecosystem, know that doing just the minimum to survive is not going to enable the partnership, nor its parent companies, to leverage their full growth potential. To really thrive, your partnership needs to continue to challenge itself to enhance its core competencies, and develop completely new ones, to successfully identify and leverage growth opportunities. This "success is a journey, not a destination" attitude will continue to keep the partnership strong and growing. After all, isn't that why you started it in the first place?

Reusing What You've Learned

In the weeks or months it has taken you to survey the land, clear away debris (or mines as the case may be), sow the topsoil, plant the seeds and nurture your partnership from defenseless seedling to semi-healthy young adulthood, something else has happened that has probably gone unnoticed: You have established a knowledge base at both partner organizations that can now be used to identify and leverage additional partnering opportunities. This intellectual capital that's been accumulated has tremendous value, and can now be reinvested for even greater returns.

Think about it – you now have templates and processes in place for assessing new partnering opportunities. The lessons you've learned should serve to make each additional partnership process more efficient and less painful than the one before. From the readiness assessment, through defining the specific partnership model, to dealing with start-up issues, your partnership project team has ridden a long learning curve. The payback for all this learning and sweat equity can and should extend well beyond the initial partnership.

A Bridge Too Few?

In his book Pegasus Bridge, author and historian Stephen Ambrose tells the tale of how a small unit of the British 6th Airborne Division, under the command of Major John Howard, secured a strategic bridge over the Caen Canal in Benouville, France in the early morning hours of June 6, 1944, hours ahead of the D-Day invasion force. The taking of Pegasus Bridge by Howard and his men constituted the very first engagement of D-Day. Control of the bridge was crucial to the Allies' sustained control of the Normandy coastline, about 3 miles away. German reinforcements, particularly their armored divisions, would need to use this bridge to reinforce the German fixed battlements along the coastline. Failure to secure and hold the bridge would have opened the invasion force to a German counterattack, which could have easily swept the Allied forces back into the sea.

Ambrose's account details the meticulous and arduous training that Howard and his select team go through in preparation for their D-Day mission. From the nighttime glider landing, to taking out the German gun placements along the bridge, to placing explosives in case the small unit was overrun by a counterattack, Howard's team rehearsed every aspect of the operation. By the time Howard and his team took off for France June 6th, they were ready to execute their plan down to the minute, and they were prepared for any number of contingencies in case the operation did not go as planned.

The mission was a resounding success. Howard and his team secured the bridge within 20 minutes of landing, and they were able to hold the bridge for several hours until reinforcements arrived. Their success will continue to be celebrated throughout history.

In the weeks following D-Day, Howard's team was dispersed into other British units. In his book, Ambrose contemplates why Howard's team, after going through such rigorous training and executing the mission with such flawless precision, was not re-deployed to capture additional strategic military targets throughout Europe. Surely there were other bridges needing to be captured and held as part of various Allied offensives that Howard and his team could have been used to secure. Despite all the well-deserved glory bestowed on Major Howard and his unit, Ambrose wonders how much more such a finely tuned team could have accomplished.

While not nearly a life-or-death drama, establishing and maintaining a profitable partnership model requires a unique skill set that can be used over and over to achieve many kinds of business objectives. And while each partnering opportunity presents its own unique set of challenges, there are certain skills that can be brought to bear on any new partnering opportunity. These skills include:

- Team Building
- Alliance Model Design
- Communications within Partnering Organizations

- Project Planning & Execution
- Issue Review & Resolution
- Establishing Performance Metrics & Monitoring

So the next time your company, and even its newly formed offspring partnership, are looking at a new market or product opportunity, your choices will again be 1) develop the new capability in-house, 2) purchase the capability from an established player, or 3) partner with another company, leveraging the strengths of both organizations to bring a unique value proposition to the marketplace. The partnering option should be much less intimidating for you as you consider these options. Collectively, you know the processes, you understand the pitfalls, you know how to make it work.

But do you know how you can take the basic partnership model to a whole new level?

Chapter 8 – Expanding Your Partnership Model

Take calculated risks. That is quite different from being rash.

George S. Patton

This book has been focused on the basics of how to qualify and build a strong and effective strategic alliance between two companies for the purpose of achieving specific business objectives. If you're reading this book, chances are that you're relatively new to the world of strategic alliances, and the one-to-one partnership model is a great place for you to start to experience the benefits that partnerships can offer.

But there are many other types of partnership models which can be used for a variety of purposes. This chapter is meant to expand your mind (without the use of hallucinogens) to consider at least one other partnership configuration to help you take advantage of future business opportunities.

As a quick review, the basic 1-1 partnership model begins by defining the answers to some basic questions:

- What is our specific growth objective?

- What is the unique value proposition we need to bring to the market to truly leverage this opportunity?

- What specific capabilities are required in order to accomplish this? Which of these do we already possess? Which do we need to develop or acquire?

- Will both partner organizations fully support and embrace this initiative, or will they start to jump ship when we hit some rough waters?

Of the questions above, all are inward focused except for the second bullet, which requires us to really understand the market we are going to approach and its various dynamics. Buyer behavior profiles and habits, current products and their attributes, substitute products, price elasticity, technology impact, service components - these market traits and others need to be analyzed in order to design and position a value proposition to buyers that truly provides us with a sustainable competitive advantage.

But what if the market opportunity under consideration was restricted to a single buyer or a very few select buyers? Could various companies join forces and form an alliance to effectively serve a single customer? The answer is YES, and the vehicle to help us navigate this new, slightly bumpier road is something I call *The Triangle Partnership Model*.

The basic premise of a *Triangle Partnership* is simply to create a true <u>'Win-Win-Win' relationship that's not based just on the price of your service or product</u>.

Triangle Partnering Model

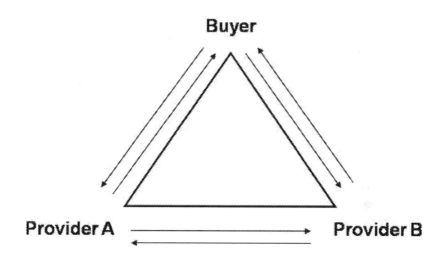

Buyer

Provider A   →   Provider B

Key Components of the Triangle Partnership Success Model

Vision
A compelling reason to share and develop a strategic vision of the possibilities

Alignment
Strategic agreement of specific goals, objectives, and expectations of results with mutual trust

Impact
Joint opportunities to leverage core capabilities through a bundled exchange of offerings

At its core, a Triangle Partnership is a shared vision, which enables all participants to exchange opportunity and influence. It is designed to create the highest level of partnership value such that all parties receive and deliver greater value than any independent offering could provide. The shared vision, beyond the business growth objectives, is to create a value proposition so compelling and differentiated that it represents a competitive advantage for ALL participants involved.

Even though the Buyer is represented at the top of the model, all participants need to be on equal footing for the partnership to be optimized. There can be none of the adversarial relationships that exist in a typical sales transactional model. <u>All parties must be willing to invest in the success of all other parties.</u> Did you catch that? The Buyer cannot sit back fat and happy when either of the Providers is not experiencing the expected full value from the partnership.

The value components of a Triangle Partnership are very similar to those of a traditional 1-1 partnership:

- Improved profitability on new business

- Compressed timeline for sales development

- New growth in non-traditional segments

- Shared risk and reduced operational costs

- Exchanging core competencies of the partner companies

- Expands opportunities and reduces cost of sales

- Enhances ability to sell at high level and receive full value for your offering

- Access to tenured relationships → lead generation

- Sharing of resources → reduced operational costs

- An expanded portfolio based on shared strategic goals, key relationships and critical business drivers.

The difference is that the value in all of these areas will be exponentially greater within a Triangle Partnership, mainly because the "marketplace" (a single customer, remember?) is invested in the success of the partnership and closely involved in critical design details. Having the Buyer become an actual participant in the alliance ensures the new enterprise never strays too far from its intended course.

Where/How Can Triangle Partnerships Be Used?

Let's look at an example of effective multi-dimensional partnering that's near and dear to my heart. All commercial and industrial facilities require many different types of maintenance and facility services. Take a typical office building. Here's just a partial list of the types of facility services required:

- Custodial

- Roof Maintenance

- Landscaping/Lawn Maintenance

- Carpet Cleaning

- Pest Control (the 6 or 8 legged kind, not the ones that send you worthless e-mails)

- HVAC

- Security – systems, personnel

- Parking Lot Repair, snow removal

- Window Washing

- Food Service – coffee stations, vending machines, cafeteria services

Those buildings sure are needy, aren't they? If your office building is like most, you have a facility manager who develops and maintains transactional (i.e., vendor) relationships with providers of each type of service required. In this type of model, each service is regarded as a separate cost item, and the facility manager does his/her best to separately beat down these providers on price. This model has been known to lead to problems, the most glaring of which is customers can receive poor service because each participating vendor can be forced to limit quality in order to turn some profit on their piece of the contract. In many cases, underpaid and under-trained workers are utilized to provide only the minimum services dictated in the contract. In short, neither "side" is exactly thrilled with doing business together, and this is certainly not a business model that you would want to write a 'white paper' on; however, it is very typical of what exists in today's facility management market.

Now let's take the Triangle Partner Model and apply it to this situation. Within this model, service providers align to provide consolidated, comprehensive facility management services. But beyond providing simple one-stop-shopping, now the service providers can partner with the buyer to design integrated levels of service that can transform the customer's facility from a cost center to a real strategic asset.

But wait! There's more. As part of the partnership, service providers now have access to many times more relationships with new customers than they ever had before. Customer acquisition costs are greatly reduced, allowing the service providers to invest more in their people and providing a higher level of quality service. Each customer becomes a new member of the partnership, with shared investment in providing optimal levels of service that can be customized to meet a set of unique needs. I know it sounds a bit utopian, but it's happening today.

The key to the success of any partner model - one-to-one, Triangle, or multi-dimensional - is that all members have a shared vision and shared investment. Which is why it's so important to select the right companies to partner with – all the due diligence we discussed in Chapter 4 will pay big dividends when you have the right partners on board.

Piecing Together the Triangle

Now before you go pitching your idea for a Triangle Partnership to senior management, know this: Triangle Partnerships can be quite a bit more work to put together and maintain than traditional partnerships (as if those aren't hard enough). As you might have inferred from the Triangle Partnership example given, the opportunity needs to be large enough to justify the initial investment associated with getting a Triangle Partnership off the ground.

So if you're contemplating this type of partnership model, please consider these factors for a successful Triangle Partnership:

- All participants must be financially sound and stable.

- You should have well-defined needs and offerings that match up to the other partners

- The proposed Triangle Partnership must create a compelling value proposition.

- All participants should have a quality reputation and strategic business fit.

- Customer bases and networks should be somewhat similar.

- There should be a viable growth opportunity for all parties.

- All parties must be willing to share short-term and long-term goals and visions.

- There needs to be a strong commitment from the senior management from all participants.

Still interested? If so, and you have a Buyer with the vision to make it work, then the Triangle Partner Model offers huge potential rewards for all participants.

Chapter 9 – Some Closing Thoughts

Patience and perseverance have a magical effect before which difficulties disappear and obstacles vanish. A little knowledge that acts is worth infinitely more than much knowledge that is idle.

John Quincy Adams

Strategic alliances and partnering models can be useful tools, but as I've said several times in this book, in the end that is all they are - tools to be used to leverage opportunities to expand your business. Too often partnerships are considered ends unto themselves, and that is a big reason why most fail – not because there was no thought put into them, but because the people behind them truly believed that by virtue of forming a partnership, good things would magically happen.

I called this book *Partnering with a Purpose* because I wanted to emphasize (you're probably sick of hearing this by now) that the business objectives must be clearly defined before even considering whether a partnership is the right way to go. Partnerships are great tools, but they're not the only tools available to grow your business. Now having said that, I will also state that with all of the various opportunities for growth open to a business today, if you are not utilizing strategic partnerships in some capacity as a part of your overall growth strategy, then you are probably missing some great opportunities.

My goals for writing *'Partnering with a Purpose'* were simple:

1. Remove the mystique around strategic alliances and get you to consider them as a viable option to grow your business.

2. Help get you started on the road to forming a strategic alliance.

3. Show you some of the do's and don'ts along the way.

Business alliances and strategic partnerships have been around for quite awhile and are here to stay. However, doing them right still seems to be a challenge. *Partnering with a Purpose* is obviously not meant to be an everything-you-need-to-know-to-form-a-successful-partnership manual. But it can be a useful guide to help you navigate around the pitfalls of trying to combine the efforts of two or more companies towards a common objective.

If, after reading this book, you believe that partnerships are too difficult and not worth the effort, then I have failed in my objective. Partnerships are not rocket science, nor even beginning science for that matter. As I said at the beginning of the book, given today's ever increasing competitive business climate, combined with the continued downsizing of most companies, more and more businesses are thinking about strategic partnerships as a new and viable business development model. Viability though, is dependent on the processes used to build and maintain the partnership. When I analyzed dozens of partnerships, the basic commonalities between successful partnerships and the commonalities between failed partnerships, seemed to jump out at me. If this book helps you to avoid making these mistakes, then it was well worth the couple hours (about my own attention span) that you've invested.

There are also many other sources you can access to learn about forming and maintaining strategic alliances. The Strategic Account Management Association (SAMA, strategicaccounts.org) and the International Facilities Management Association (IFMA.org) provide an abundance of resources on partnerships and current partnering opportunities. I encourage you to take a look at their web sites and even attend one of their many educational events.

Remember, at the end of the day, people do business with people, and the strategic partnering approach is all about accessing and leveraging the core competencies and tenured relationships that exist within both organizations to offer a better value proposition than either partner could provide alone. Never forget that your partner is a true extension of your team, so treat them as you would another employee or associate. Involve them in your operations, keep no hidden agendas, and expect the same from them.

Finally, have fun! Forming an alliance is a tremendous venture, one that offers ample opportunities to meet new people, develop new skills, and conduct business as you never have before. It's my hope that you take full advantage of these opportunities, and remember: if the day-to-day grind ever gets you down - you've got a partner.

Dave Koester

Acknowledgments

When you stop and really think about it, life presents us with one partnering opportunity after another; from birth through ones' career to retirement and beyond, we are always faced with partnering decisions. At birth we automatically partner with our parents and in school we partner with our teachers and begin forging partnerships with friends. Then as we mature, most of us enter into a special partnering relationship with our spouse which often results in partnering opportunities with our children. Throughout our careers, we all make a series of partnering decisions, with companies, employers, co-workers, customers, etc. and often this landscape changes frequently based on the strength of those partnering commitments. The structure and results of these many partnering relationships define who we are, our character, our legacy, our reputation and how we will all be remembered.

To my family, Carol, Brian, Rob and Sharon…I can't thank you enough for your support, encouragement and patience over the years. I know at times, it was a crazy ride, but I think we all are better off today because of everything we have been through together.

To my parents…who gave me enough rope to hang myself, but always supported me through the good times and the bad. I wish you were still here today to celebrate with me. I especially want to thank my Dad, for teaching me early on how to work with people and the basic sales and communication skills that ultimately shaped my career.

To my close friends… especially Mark and Jim. You have made a difference in my life! I thank you for your support, your love, and your confidence and most importantly, for always being there. Besides this book, just think of the many chapters and stories we have written together over the years and we're not done yet! Ugotaluvit.

To my readers…I can't thank you enough for making the investment and taking the time to read this book. I sincerely hope that you enjoy the read and that you are able to take away some ideas and concepts to make your partnering experiences even better.

To my business partner Charley…a special thanks for hanging in there with me for the last ten years. It has been a labor of love and I am forever grateful for your support.

To Matthew Kelly (Author of The Dream Manager)…thank you for your encouragement, your counsel, your direction and being a sounding board for me as I navigated the world of publishing. You were instrumental in helping me make my final decision.

To Bob Carter…thanks for your support, friendship, encouragement and believing in 'Partnering with a Purpose'. You were the final push to make this a reality!

Remember, *Partnering with a Purpose* can have application to all aspects of your life. Take the time to make the right investments in all of your partnerships and something wonderful will happen!

About the Author

As President & CEO of a full-service consultancy firm, Dave Koester has over 30 years of sales, marketing and business development experience within the service sector, energy and facility management, foodservice and food processing industries. In addition, Dave has also spent over the last twelve years of his professional career enhancing and refining the art of strategic partnering and business alliance development. Prior to starting The Koester Group, LLC in 1997, Dave held numerous middle and senior management positions with several leading Fortune 500 companies such as, Ecolab, S.C. Johnson, DiverseyLever, FirstEnergy Corp., Orkin and Procter & Gamble, just to name a few. Then, in the fall of 2000, Dave joined forces with two other top industry professionals who shared his vision, as they combined their collective skills and experience to create *The Linkage Group, LLC.* In 2008 and 2009, Dave served as the Director of Sales & Marketing for Victory Industrial Products LLC, taking the company from a regional concern with one manufacturing facility to a national player with three manufacturing locations and in 2010 served as the Director of Corporate Business Development for Premier MSS – a Voith Industrial Services Company before returning once again to his consulting practice.

Over the course of the last twelve years, Dave has focused his consulting efforts almost exclusively on the facility management, energy/utility sectors and related value-added services. In working with the senior management teams of IES, EMCOR, Encompass and FirstEnergy Corp., Dave designed and engineered several major new initiatives for these companies that allowed them to differentiate their total offering, thereby offering an expanded portfolio of products and services to their growing customer base. The programs developed included: **Triangle Partnering** – which blends the capabilities of three different partners, **Total Customer Solutions** - which focused on Performance Contracting, Asset Management and Financing; **Facility Management Solutions** - which added the facility management and building services piece to the offering, and the **FirstEnergy Facility Management Alliance** – which combined the offerings of 10 industry leading service companies, via strategic partnering, to allow FirstEnergy to offer total consolidation on all products and related services to selected customers.

In addition, Dave also has extensive experience as a sales trainer and public speaker, conducting many seminars on consultative sales techniques, negotiation skills, team building, solution selling and change management. Utilizing his extensive background and industry knowledge in the Integrated Pest Management field, Dave has also been called upon to be the keynote speaker at several national sales meetings and networking conferences within that industry. He has been a member of IFMA (International Facility Management Association), the IFMA Consultants Council and is currently a member of SAMA (Strategic Account Management Association) and the IAOP (International Association of Outsourcing Professionals).

Dave attended Thomas More College and Xavier University in the Cincinnati, Ohio area, majoring in Natural Science (Biology / Chemistry) and also selected courses in Engineering at the University of Kentucky. He also received AIB Certification in Food Plant Sanitation and HACCP Program Development. Dave, his wife Carol, and their family reside in Cincinnati, Ohio.